Hebridean Pioneers

HEBRIDEAN PIONEERS

MALCOLM A. MACQUEEN

Selkirk
STORIES

ISBN 978-1-926494-34-0

Originally published in 1957.
Hebridean Pioneers is in the public domain.
Introduction copyright © 2019 by John Westlie

Selkirk Stories™ and the image of a heart with three stars are trademarks of Selkirk Stories, Cornwall, Prince Edward Island, Canada.

Table of Contents

Introduction	vii
Foreword	1
Early Scottish Emigration	2
Selkirk Sponsors Settlement on Prince Edward Island	5
Education	50
The Church	78
Mills	93
Lumbering	102
Hunting	104
Fishing	105
Ships and Seafaring	108
Dr. Angus Macaulay	123
Names of Settlers, 1811	142
Origin of the Name Belfast	148
Robert Jones	152
Settlers in Lots 49 and 50	156
Joseph Beers, Esq.	158
James L. Hayden	159
William Jetson	163
John Burho	163
John Eachern	164
James Laird	165
John Praught	166
John Van Niderstine	166
Peter Musick	166
The Enmans of Vernon River	168

Martins of Newtown River	170
Munros of Alberry Plans	173
Nicholson of Orwell Cove and Orwell River	176
Descendants of Rev. William Macqueen in Orwell	180
Peter Alexander Macqueen of Townsville, Australia	188
Dr. Malcolm Macqueen and Col. Thomas Potter Macqueen, M.P. of Bedfordshire, England	190
Robertsons and Fergusons of Marshfield, P.E.I.	196
Tweedy and Irving Families	199
Index of Names	202

INTRODUCTION

On August 6, 1953, the eve of the day 150 years earlier when the first of the Earl of Selkirk's three ships of Scottish settlers landed in nearby Orwell Cove, Saint John's Presbyterian Church in Belfast, Prince Edward Island, held a commemoration of the historic event. To judge from the Charlottetown *Guardian* article reporting on the celebration, Malcolm Macqueen was the highlight of the evening. He is featured in both the headline and the first paragraph of the *Guardian* article, and the entirety of his speech is quoted. Malcolm Macqueen was clearly seen as the undisputed authority on all matters related to Scottish immigration to Prince Edward Island.

Macqueen acquired this authority over forty years of research, publication and constant communication with the community in and around Belfast. His first book, *Skye Pioneers and "The Island"* (1929), is, if not the first, then among the first publications on immigration from the Scottish Highlands to Canada. It presents a nostalgic look back at the early settlements and an exalted view of the contributions made by Scottish immigrants to the founding institutions of Canada. However, it shows signs of hasty composition, with redundant sections and clear evidence that the book was put into its final form between mid-August 1929, when Macqueen returned from an extended voyage to the British Isles, and late December of the same year, when the first reviews of the book appear in newspapers. *Hebridean Pioneers* shows none of this haste. Carefully written and well documented, it is rich in the kind of source material historians and genealogists seek: names, facts, dates and places. Yet *Hebridean Pioneers* is far less cited than Macqueen's earlier work, and less often consulted.

When Malcolm Macqueen left Prince Edward Island for Queen's University in Ontario in 1900, then made his way west to Winnipeg after his graduation in 1903, his sights were set on making money. A 1901 letter from Maggie Macphail Jenkins to her brother John Andrew (later Sir Andrew) Macphail gives a glimpse into the young Macqueen's fascination with wealth and prestige:

> We were very much amused at M. McQueen's account of you ... I have not space to go over half of what he said, but ... he gave the people here an *earache* on the subject. He speaks of Georgie [Mrs. Macphail] in hushed tones as the '*kindest and best looking rich woman*' in the *world*, I think it was. ... "He's awful rich" etc. etc.

Within a few years, Macqueen would have the same things he so admired: wealth, a grand house and a rich wife. Macqueen arrived in Winnipeg during the real estate boom of the early years of the twentieth century. While he read law with the firm of Munro and Mackenzie, qualifying as a solicitor in 1906 and as a barrister in 1908, he appears to have made his money in real estate, not in the practice of law. In the years between 1908 and 1911, all evidence points to Macqueen's acquiring significant wealth. A social column in the February 9, 1911, edition of the Winnipeg *Free Press* tells us that "M. A. Macqueen ... leaves tonight for a month's holiday trip to California and Hawaii." The next year Macqueen married the daughter of Robert T. Riley, one of the wealthiest and most prominent businessmen in Winnipeg. Macqueen had a house built for himself and his bride in one of Winnipeg's most elegant neighbourhoods at a cost that puts the house in the top third of Winnipeg real estate prices for the period. He and Mrs. Macqueen later lived with Robert T. Riley in an even more stately home in the elegant Armstrong's Point neighbourhood, building another house nearby when Mr. Riley died in 1944. Macqueen had achieved a life of wealth and social standing, but one at odds with the austerity and self-denial of his ancestors that he evokes in *Skye Pioneers* and praises in his 1953 speech.

But Malcolm Macqueen retired in 1918, when he was forty years old. He apparently had acquired enough wealth in investments and real estate to turn his time and energy from the pursuit of money to research into his ancestors and the history of his native province. *Skye Pioneers*, his first book, is widely consulted, even today, by researchers. *Hebridean Pioneers*, published almost thirty years later, is the crowning achievement of Macqueen's career but is far less frequently cited in other publications. It may have been less widely distributed and acknowledged because Macqueen's health was failing by the time it was published in 1957. Malcolm Macqueen died three years later, after what his obituary calls a long illness. His ashes were interred in the Old Kildonan Cemetery in Winnipeg, a burying ground established by the other group of Selkirk Settlers, those whom the Earl of Selkirk brought to the Red River Valley in 1812.

This edition seeks to make *Hebridean Pioneers* more widely available with a reformatted, easy-to-read text. This edition is the first to include an index of the names included in *Hebridean Pioneers*. We hope it is of use to those seeking information about their ancestors or the history of Scottish immigration to Canada.

John Westlie
Meadowbank, Prince Edward Island, 2019

Foreword

Emigrants from the Highlands and Western Isles of Scotland hold a conspicuous place among Canadian pioneers. Of these hardy people a representative group settled in Belfast, Prince Edward Island, in 1803. There, for over a century, they lived in almost complete isolation. Neighbor married neighbor, thereby assuring a culture as purely Celtic as that of their forebears. Ancestral traditions and beliefs continued to influence their daily lives and were taken for granted much as were the seasons. Thus were preserved the distinctive ways of the Gael with all its unpredictable diversity. Now the isolation is gone. Intermarriage with outsiders is changing the character of the people and for the most part those of the present generation display a lamentable lack of interest in the past. But the past is a priceless heritage and the story of fortitude and faith during the years of trial in the wilderness of Belfast should not be forgotten.

Anatole France once wrote "Let us not lightly cast aside anything that belongs to the Past, for only with the Past can we rear the fabric of the Future."

A narrative of events in the early days in Belfast may arouse an interest in what was meritorious in the lives of their ancestors. Descendants of these pioneers may, perhaps, be forgiven if in an attempt to recall something of their life, manners and achievements they applaud "with partial fondness" their many virtues, for as the great Gibbon once observed, "Personal merit can alone deserve the notice of posterity."

Early Scottish Emigration

Individual Scottish Highlanders arrived in the American colonies at an early date. For instance, Matthew Grant, ancestor of President Grant, is said to have settled in Dorchester, Massachusetts, in 1630. However it was much later before they began to emigrate in groups. They had a settlement in the Cape Fear River region of North Carolina in 1729. Some say they were there in 1715. The destruction of the clan system at Culloden, in 1746, was followed by a long period of economic distress and social unrest. The chief, no longer a petty monarch, as in fact he had been for ages, required no defenders. The tenant thus lost his age-long privilege of military and other service in return for low rents. The landlords converted large areas into grazing land and deer forests. These methods gave the landlord greater returns, but, unfortunately for the tenants, required fewer hands. The tenants thus faced the hard lot of those driven by penury from the land which their forebears had occupied for generations and which they regarded as their own. The clansmen surveyed the future with bewilderment and anxiety. Where were they to go? What were they to do? Thousands walked to the Lowlands where they got work on farms and in factories. For those who could afford it, emigration with its prospect of free land, offered an appealing answer. So, with what was realized from the sale of their scanty worldly goods, many abandoned the land of their nativity and sought new homes in the vast primeval forests of America.

The *Scots Magazine* for September, 1769, records that 54 vessels full of emigrants from the Western Isles and the Highlands sailed for North Carolina between April and July, 1770. It is said that up to this time no emigrant from Skye had gone anywhere other than to North Carolina. In 1771 James Macdonald[1], merchant, Portree, and Norman Macdonald[2] of Slate, for themselves and on behalf of Hugh Macdonald[3], Edmund Macqueen, John Betton, and Alex. Macqueen of Slate, the Rev. Mr. William Macqueen[4] and Alexander

---

1   Speaboat, tacksman.
2   Scalpa, tacksman.
3   Armadale, grandson of Sir James Macdonald, Chief.
4   Minister of Snizort.

Macdonald[1] of the said Island of Skye petitioned the "King's Majesty in Council" for a grant of forty thousand acres of land in North Carolina upon the usual terms and conditions of such grants. The petition was dismissed, 19th June, 1772, by the Privy Council Committee on Plantation Affairs, on the ground that it was not desirable that so many people should leave the country. But this refusal did not lessen the eager desire for homes in America. By this time the flood was so great as to excite public alarm. The famous writer, Dr Samuel Johnson, on his memorable tour of the Highlands and Islands of Scotland in 1773, in company with his biographer, Boswell, was struck by the magnitude of the exodus and the choleric old Doctor was moved to refer to it as the "Epidemic fury of emigration." The case of Skye is characteristic and gives a picture of what was taking place in the Highlands and Islands generally.

The Revolutionary War put a temporary stop to the exodus to North Carolina. But the various Highland colonies there were well established, and as soon as peace was made, people in the homeland began to join their kinsfolk overseas, regardless of the political separation from the motherland.

---

1   Cuidrach, tacksman.

Selkirk Sponsors Settlement on Prince Edward Island

By the turn of the 19th century, public opinion in the Lowlands was aroused by the alarming depopulation of the Highlands. Among those moved by the distress in that remote region was the romantic Scottish nobleman, Thomas Douglas, 5th Earl of Selkirk. In 1805 he published a volume entitled "Observations on the Present State of the Highlands of Scotland with a view of the causes and probable consequences of Emigration." In this work he reveals his reasons for sponsoring the settlement on Prince Edward Island, in 1803. Selkirk wrote:

> Without any immediate or local connection with the Highlands, I was led, very early in life, to take a warm interest in the fate of my countrymen in that part of the kingdom. During my academical studies, my curiosity was strongly excited by the representations I had heard of the antient state of society, and the striking peculiarity of manners still remaining among them; and, in the year 1792, I was prompted to take an extensive tour through their wild region and to explore many of its remotest and most secluded valleys.

I learned that the Highlanders were dispersing to a variety of situations, in a foreign land, where they were lost not only to their native country, but to themselves as a separate people. Admiring many generous and manly features in their character, I could not observe without regret the rapid decline of their genuine manners, to which the circumstances of the country seemed inevitably to lead. I thought, however, that a portion of the antient spirit might be preserved among the Highlanders of the New World—that the emigrants might be brought together in some part of our own colonies, where they would be of national utility, and where no motives of general policy would militate (as they certainly may at home) against the preservation of all those peculiarities of customs and language, which they are themselves so reluctant to give up, and which are perhaps intimately connected with many of their most striking and characteristic virtues.

Selkirk tried to interest the national government in diverting emigration from the American states to the British colonies in a large way. But "seeing no probability of my views being adopted by Government, and reluctant to abandon the object altogether, I was led to consider how far, under the encouragement held out, I could, as an individual, follow it up on a more limited scale, to the effect at least of establishing the practicability of my suggestion. Having, therefore, received the assurance of a grant of land on liberal terms, such as promised an adequate return of the unavoidable expenses of the undertaking, I resolved to try the experiment, and, at my own risk, to engage some of the emigrants, who were preparing to go to the United States, to change their destination, and embark for our own colonies." But Selkirk met constant opposition, and when preparations were well advanced, he learned that "in consequence of some calumnious reports, Government were disposed to look less favorably than at first on my undertaking."

His Lordship's representations to the Government removed "the grounds of these misapprehensions" but he "was given to understand, however, that it would be more satisfactory to Government, if the people I had engaged were settled in a Maritime situation, instead that I had at first in contemplation. For reasons, which I may perhaps have occasion hereafter to lay before the public, I was by no means satisfied that this suggestion was founded in just views of national policy. Nevertheless I thought it my duty under all the circumstances of the case, to acquiesce, and determined on making my settlement in Prince

Edward's Island, in the Gulf of St. Lawrence."

Although he settled a few families in the Townships of Dover and Chatham in Upper Canada, Selkirk turned to Prince Edward Island, that gem in the ocean, bought a tract of about sixty thousand or more acres of land, and there launched the largest and most successful of all his ventures in colonization.

In the volume already referred to, Selkirk writes of these events as follows:

> When these general principles are understood, the part which I have myself taken, in regard to the settlers whom I conveyed, in 1803, to Prince Edward's Island, will need little explanation. Of these settlers the greatest proportions were from the Isle of Skye; a district which had so decided a connection with North Carolina, that no emigrants had ever gone from it to any other quarter. There were a few others from Ross-shire, from the north part of Argyllshire, and from some interior districts in Inverness-shire, all of whose connexions lay in some part of the United States. There were some also from a part of the Island of Uist, where the emigration had not taken a decided direction.
>
> If my views had extended no further than the mere improvement of a property in the

colony I have mentioned, I might, without any loss, and with much less trouble, have found settlers enough in the districts where the custom of emigrating to the same quarter was already established. But this was not my purpose. I had undertaken to settle these lands with emigrants whose views were directed towards the United States; and, without any wish to increase the general spirit of emigration, I could not avoid giving more than ordinary advantages to those who should join me. The prejudices entertained against the situation I proposed, were industriously fomented by some persons who had conceived a jealousy against my undertaking; and, in consequence of this obstruction, I found it necessary to extend my offers of encouragement as far as I could, without a total disregard of my own interest.

The difficulties in organizing an expedition of eight hundred people are great at any time and place; in the isolated Highlands a century and a half ago it was colossal. A trip thither meant an arduous journey of many days on foot, horseback, or by carriage.

Finally, after much negotiation all was ready, and in the summer of 1803, eight hundred and three Highland souls, "fearing neither the rage of the ocean, nor the hardships of uncivilized life," bade farewell to friends and country and embarked on the ships *Polly*, *Dykes* and *Oughton* to cross the Western Main. These were not evicted tenants. All left home of their own free will and almost all on their own resources, the chief compulsion being a desire to improve their lot in life. After an uneventful voyage, the *Polly*, which sailed from Portree, arrived in Orwell Bay, Prince Edward Island, on Sunday, August 7. Her complement, as Selkirk records in his diary, was "250 full passengers and nearly 400 souls." The majority of these passengers were from the Isle of Skye. All were members or adherents of the Presbyterian church, and all but a few, who bought land near Tryon, settled in Belfast.

The *Dykes*, with Selkirk on board, arrived in Charlottetown two days after the *Polly*, "the Skye ship," as Selkirk described her in his diary.

The *Oughton* arrived on August 27 with forty or fifty families from the Island of Uist. These were Roman Catholics. They settled on Selkirk's land in the vicinity of Three Rivers, or, as the district is known today, Georgetown.

Thus concluded one of the largest systematic migrations sponsored by an individual of which up to that time there is any record. It stimulated Highland emigration, especially to the Isles of Prince Edward and Cape Breton; so much so that in the first six years of the nineteenth century ten thousand Highlanders migrated to North America, chiefly to that part known today as the Maritime Provinces, according to a pamphlet published in Edinburgh by one Robert Browne.

America was still in the days of its virgin grandeur. Forests of stately pine, spruce, balsam, hemlock, beech, birch and maple stretched as far as the eye could see. Never again would the natural beauty of the continent match the prospect spread before the eyes of these weary settlers on that autumn day of 1803. But when they set foot on shore there were neither friends to receive them, nor homes to give them shelter. Except for a few Loyalist settlers on the north side of Orwell Bay and along Vernon River, the country around them was an unbroken, melancholy wilderness. The forest seemed interminable.

The landing was made a little west of the present Halliday's Wharf, on a farm that had been taken up by a U.E. Loyalist officer named MacMillan and that has remained in the family to the present day. A small colony of French had spent some years in the vicinity, but had abandoned the district and returned to France after the fall of Louisburg, in 1758. The land they had cleared was now hidden by a new growth of spruce, a tree that reproduces itself very rapidly on the Island. In the French burying ground, near the landing place, still stood markers of native sandstone, bearing the initials of the departed.

A passing picture of pioneer life in those days and of the courage with which immigrants faced its loneliness and hardships may be found in Selkirk's account of the two squatters he met in Belfast on his arrival there.

> Fraser—a semi-Highlander—squatter on Lot 57—son of a soldier—Loyalist—an infant when his father formerly settled in N. York, came to the island—now little above 25—set down in June 1801, and cleared a small spot—planted 5 bushels of Potatoes, but the crop failed and he had not 20 of return—in 1802 he planted 12 bushels, had about 100 of crop, but for want of accommodation to preserve them lost most of them, he has now a good appearance of crop, has planted 16 bushels of Potatoes, 1-½ bu. of Wheat—1 Barley— with some Indian Corn and Turnips. By pacing his clearance may be 3-½ or 4 acres—say 1-½ or 2 pots[1], 1-¼ wheat—½ acre barley—¼ acre of other things. This crop must put him out of reach of want. He has of Cattle, a Bull, 4 Cows, 1 of which yield[2], 2 year olds— 4 calves—cuts

---

1   Potatoes.
2   Not giving milk.

about 12 ton hay. McLeod another squatter has about 2 acres cleared on which he has 12 bushels potatoes planted. Being small wood, he cut it in about 6 days—he is a good axeman—has been long in America—he was about 6 days putting up his house. He only began last Spring and had not proceeded far when he heard of the Sale of the Lot and the Colony coming out, which checked him in his improvements—he has not yet built a chimney to his house, etc. He, however, is proposing to go on with that and other improvements, on my promising that if he does not get the land he is on, he shall have an allowance for his improvements—with which promise he seems quite satisfied.

In his diary Selkirk records that "The *Polly* has had a remarkably quick passage and arrived on Sunday. I wish she had rather been a little after than before me. From this circumstance the people are to land without any preparation for their reception on an uninhabited spot. Had I been a week sooner, some kind of barracks might have been ready. They are, however, setting about hutting themselves in whigwams."

Before going to Belfast, Selkirk spent four days in Charlottetown, calling on government officials and attending to business affairs. In 1803 this village had only 72 houses. "Before setting out," he writes, "I agreed with the McMillans & McFee to build a log house 25 × 16, roofed so as to stand this winter, for which they are to have £5 & promise to finish it in 10 days—this is for a storehouse."

McPhee lived at China Point, on the north side of Orwell Bay. Descendants reside on the ancestral lands today. The place name is derived from that of an early settler named Cheney, probably U.E. Loyalist.

On the evening of August 13, Selkirk arrived in Belfast. He "found that the people had already lodged themselves in temporary wigwams, constructed after the fashion of the Indians, by setting up a number of poles in a conical form, tied together at top, and covered with boughs of trees. Those of the spruce fir were preferred and, when disposed in regular layers of sufficient thickness, formed a very substantial thatch, giving a shelter not inferior to that of a tent."

As these pioneers kept neither records, diaries nor private papers, for very few were equipped to do so, little would be known of life in Belfast in those early days, especially of housing, but for Selkirk's voluminous diaries and his correspondence with his agent in Belfast, Dr. Angus Macaulay. From these sources we learn that as soon as each family had selected and was allotted land, they started to build log cabins instructed by McMillan and McPhee. These log structures were easily built, strong, warm and comfortable during the bitter Island winters.

In his entry of August 15 Selkirk records that "Mr. McEachern, the Catholic priest, says their houses the first year should be about 12 ft. square, or as small as they can do with—as the first houses that are built are seldom found to be well situated or to serve much purpose afterwards—therefore build them slight to get them quick and easily done and take time for chusing a good situation and building substantially a year or two after, recommends covering with boards, and etc., sawing with whipsaw—shingles are expensive for the first beginning, requiring many nails," and "Chimneys here are one of the most expensive parts of common houses. Mr. Hartz, Mason, reckons five days of a mason and two labourers to building one. Four or five days of a labourer quarrying stones—besides carrying—thus a chimney cannot be under four pounds. They are usually built open and wide. Very few people use stoves and those who do of iron—"

Here we may digress in order to make clear the type of dwelling built by the early settlers. After being on the Island from August 9 Selkirk set out for Halifax on September 17. The following appears in his diary under that date:

After an unfavorable morning, the day clearing up, I left Charlotte Town about 2 o'clock accompanied by Mr. Stewart the Sheriff who came over out of compliment and also Mr. Ross, Minister of Pictou and Mr. Wright son of the Surveyor General who took passage expecting to meet Mr. C. with the tent I had sent for and to encamp on some part of the shore being too late for Pictou. The tent did not arrive, so that after passing Point Prim as the night was coming on we made for the new settlement begun by Angus Beaton & Co. which we made about dark. His party consisting of four families are still in their whigwams in which I had reckoned on finding shelter but as they are not very clean, & the night was fine it was determined to encamp in the usual style of woodsmen under the canopy of heaven wrapped in thick great coats & upon a layer of spruce boughs opposite to a great fire. This was the accommodation of all the rest of the Party, but I was luxurious and having brought a hammock and blanket it was slung between two trees and I lay there half undressed, and four poles were placed across one another to support a kind of curtain over my head—this tent or curtain was another hammock which Mr. Stewart refused to make use of. The night began fine, but about one o'clock came on thick, and a little rain beginning we decamped and took to the boat with an Ebb-tide down the Straights.

Angus Beaton's party have got up the walls and spars of the roofs of two log houses— one we saw 13 feet by 10 and very tolerably done, without any assistance or instructions, but seeing the storehouse going on at Belfast, five men were only two days in doing one of them, tho' raw axemen. They had great baskets of Lobsters, two or three of which they boiled for us—these the children pick up along the rocks on the shore.

Sunday, 18th. Daylight found us very near the spot where I first landed on the Island; we continued with the Ebb along shore towards Wood Islands, under a high shore apparently much better land than we had landed upon farther west. The Ebb being spent before we reached the Islands we landed to breakfast, at a cove, where kindling a fire we brought out our cold pork, and also boiled steaks, and etc., and took a hearty meal.

Leaving about 8 o'clock Selkirk reached Pictou at dark.

But to return to the chronicle of the early days in Belfast:

After spending a few busy days among the settlers, Selkirk left for Charlottetown, for there was much to do. The 1802 "harvest had been unproductive," and provisions were scarce and difficult to get. To make matters worse, Capt. Darby had failed to bring the oatmeal as promised. The situation might have been uncomfortable but for the fact that "a schooner from Pictou was at the harbour's mouth with 90 barrels of flour bought on speculation, but going away for want of sale. This was purchased at 10 dollars a barrel and will secure us till harvest or till the arrival of the *Bess* from New York."

Selkirk returned to Charlottetown by way of Vernon River. He landed on the east bank a short distance above the site of the present Vernon River Bridge, and visited James Laird, a Scottish Loyalist, from Carolina, who had settled in Vernon River in 1795. Selkirk formed a high opinion of this man, and received valuable advice and help from him. He seems to have been cruelly treated by those who should have been his protectors, but he harbored no bitter memories of his persecutors. Selkirk records these events in his diary under date of Monday, August 15, 1803.

I went up Orwell Bay in a boat to Vernon River and had a glance of the upper part of Lot 57 where three or four settlers have taken possession of the best spots: Went up to J. Laird's in Vernon River—a Loyalist Settler from Carolina who lent me a horse and agreed to show me the way to Charlottetown—he began here quite bare 8 years ago—has now 50 acres cleared, much upland hay, a good stock of sheep and cattle, an orchard, a comfortable house, and plenty of everything—he values his improvements at £400—he has 200 acres assigned him as a Loyalist—Laird had been formerly settled on another lot, but after nine years of toil, it was discovered that by a mistake of the surveyors he was set down on a lot that was not his own and was obliged to move, without receiving any compensation for his improvements. He does not seem at an end of his troubles, for last year the Gov. (now proprietor of this general lot) brought an action of Ejectment on an allegation of a similar error tho' L. says he holds a patent signed by the Gov. himself—the Ch. Justice, however, checked the proceedings and would not allow the action to proceed. Laird alleges that the G's motive for this was because he had dunned him for a rent due for a farm which was let to the Gov. by an absentee proprietor (Loyalist also) who had appointed Laird his agent—Mr. Throckmorton[1] of Cherry Valley. This farm he had held 7 years—the rent promised £5 p. ann. and not yet paid—the Governor has now left it, everything gone to ruin tho' bound to keep it in repair— this is Laird's acct; the farm, fences, etc., I saw as I passed and they are certainly in a shockingly neglected state. L. says the Gov. was always very friendly to him till he demanded the rent. This farm of 5 or 600 acres and 100 or 80 at least clear—a good house, orchard and mill is the same that Jo. Stewart told me was on sale and might be got for about £300—

The road from Laird's is for some distance a mere track—passes behind some good settlements and considerable clearings. Along Vernon River are a considerable number of Loyalist allotments, and their clearing, joining each other give some extent to the prospect—there is a continued track of clearing in this way near the Saw Mill at the head of tidewater. Laird reckons 7 proprietors and 4 tenants on Lot 50—the proprietors are all on Loyalist allotments. These allotments have perhaps been more

---

[1] A Loyalist officer in the Revolutionary War.

generally taken up here, on account of the navigable water—

Leaving the head of tidewater on the Vernon, he traveled along the trail now known as the Town Road. The country was practically wilderness. Today, with the exception of a few acres on each farm reserved for firewood, the whole countryside is under cultivation. Fields of grain, timothy, potatoes and turnips meet the eye on every side. Pastures of lush grass provide a rich living for herds of well-bred dairy cattle. The farms, generally, are of one hundred acres, each with comfortable dwelling and tidy, well-kept outbuildings. Almost every farm is crossed by a creek, crystal clear, that brings comfort to man and beast.

Benjamin Chappell, first postmaster of Charlottetown, kept an interesting diary, in which he records that Selkirk, on Sept. 9, arranged with George Hobbs, George Bagnall, James MacDonald, and Theophilus Chappell for the erection of another building 18 × [?], for which they were to be paid £45. On September 17, Selkirk left for Halifax, and on October 17th Chappell acknowledged that he was paid by Selkirk's agent Williams.

While the Earl was engrossed in these affairs, "an alarming contagious fever broke out," he writes, "and gave me no small degree of anxiety, by its progress among the settlers. My apprehensions, however, were relieved by the presence and assistance of a medical gentleman, whom I was fortunate enough to have as my companion, and whose professional skill was equalled only by his amiable and humane attention to every class of patients. Through his assiduous and unremitted exertions, the disease was soon alleviated; and few fatal cases occured. There were not many of the settlers, however, that escaped the contagion altogether; it was difficult to intercept it among people living in such close vicinity, and in an continual intercourse which no means could be found for preventing. This fever had been occasioned by some accidental importation, and certainly not by the climate, which is remarkably healthy. The disease was nearly eradicated when the people began to disperse to their separate lots, upon which they had all begun to work before the middle of September." Elsewhere we learn from Selkirk's notes that the medical gentleman was Dr. John Shaw, Jun. He was living in Annapolis, Maryland, between 1803-5.

Many letters passed between Selkirk and his agent, in Belfast, Dr. Angus Macaulay, during these days, and a variety of subjects, including milk cows, grains, coal for the blacksmith, and boards were mentioned.

[Addressed to Dr. Macaulay]

Charlotte Town
Friday 2nd Sept.

Dear Sir:—

I am likely to be detained here some days. I shall send the canoe back and forward daily, and beg you will send me each time a single line to mention how things are going on, and anything material that requires my attention.

The MacMillans and MacFee have, I believe, some Barley ripe and cut down, but they must be too busy to thresh. I beg you, however, to purchase it for me on the foot at 3/6 per bushel—cash—as well as any that is at Fraught's, Enmans & Fraser's and to employ some of our own people to thresh it out on my account. I can get it ground into meal immediately which will be a reasonable supply of cheaper provisions for the people. The flat with the flour and meal will go down tomorrow early.

Yours,
Selkirk

PS. Jasper has the keys in a paper parcel for you.

Although some things were overlooked, Selkirk saw to it that one of the most useful craftsmen in building a new community came out with the settlers. This was the skilled blacksmith, Charles MacWilliam, of Kirkcudbright, who was on the same ship as Selkirk himself. He, and his descendants, have played a worthy part in the life of Belfast. Selkirk engaged MacWilliam on the following terms:

St. Mary's Isle[1]
April 16, 1803

In settling with Charles MacWilliam, you are to allow his annual money wages at the rate of Thirty pounds, besides which, he is to have two cows kept for him, ground for planting five hundred-weight of potatoes, two stone of wool, and a hundred stone of meal. His bargain is to continue for three years from Whitsunday, if his conduct continues as satisfactory as hitherto.

Selkirk

To MacWilliam

---

[1] Selkirk's home in Kirkcudbrightshire.

P.S. If at the expiry of his service, C. MacW. wishes to return to this country, he is to be conveyed free of expense.

From Kirkcudbright also came James Williams, perhaps the most colorful character in the whole group. He had served in the army at Quebec and elsewhere and, on discharge, had returned to his native country, where he may have been a neighbor of Selkirk's. At any rate, Selkirk met him and was so impressed by his fitness to further his schemes of colonization, that he sent him into the Highlands to recruit emigrants for the proposed settlement. The work suited his talents, for he possessed a magnetic personality. With vivid stories of the favorable climate and vast natural resources awaiting the grasp of the first settlers, he inspired many with his own enthusiasm for emigration.

Williams appears to have been authorized to sell Selkirk's lands in Belfast. That excellent newspaper, *The Guardian*, of Charlottetown, of which the enlightened editor is Mr. Frank Walker, in the issue of December 21, 1954, published a copy of a contract of sale from James Williams, as agent for Selkirk, to James Munn and Malcolm Munn, farmers, of two hundred acres of land extending forty chains along the road from Pinette to Wood Islands. The contract was made at Charlottetown, on February 24, 1807. This document is in possession of Edgar Munn, great grandson of James, who lives on the ancestral homestead at Belle Creek. James Munn died on June 5, 1867, aged 84. The Munns, and their neighbors, Mac-Millans, Shaws and others, came from the island Colonsay in 1806 on the ship *Spencer*.

It would be too much to expect complete harmony in so large a group. One is, therefore, not surprised to learn from Selkirk's diary that unrest smoldered among the settlers from the day they landed. Some were, with good reason as we now know, dissatisfied with the quality of the soil, others with their location.

But Selkirk was not discouraged. He looked to the future with confidence. Not content with what he had already done, he was planning to bring out more settlers, as the following memorandum reveals.

> J. W. to allow Dond. Nicholson (Steinshole) £20 for free passage to Scotland, and if he brings out settlers 6d. per acre on what they take up — to promise this verbally without giving any writing, I to advise D. N. when in Scotland as to chartering, not answering for anything till half freight paid — if land procured for them at Three Rivers to give J. W. notice 4 to 6 weeks.

It may not be amiss to add a word as to the use of the term *Steinshole*. He belonged to the tacksman class. A tacksman held his farm as tenant from the chief, from whom some were descended and others closely related. They, in turn, leased to several sub-tenants, who tilled the soil. The tacksman's position was akin to that of the holder of the manor in England. They were the gentry in the Highlands and were usually commissioned officers in the army. They took the name of their farm, such as, Kingsburgh, Cuidrach, Steinshole, and so forth. Thus, the tacksman of Steinshole, Donald Nicholson, would be known as Nicholson of Steinshole, or simply Steinshole. He was always so called in Orwell. He was a descendant of Rev. Donald Nicholson, M.A., Chief of the Nicholsons of Scorrybreck, Skye.

Writing of his trip up Vernon River, Selkirk refers to Steinshole: "This day's expedition was in two wooden canoes in which, besides Mr. Shaw and Dr. Macaulay, were Steinshole, and Roderick McKenzie, the two principal men of the Skye and Ross-shire parties with three or four inferior people as boatsmen—"

In remuneration for his help in inducing settlers to come to Prince Edward Island, Selkirk gave Steinshole the farm of about two hundred acres lying on both banks of Orwell River and extending from tide-water easterly about one and one-half miles to Murray Harbor Road. A few years later, after living in the meantime with his parents, Mr. and Mrs. John Nicholson, in Orwell Cove, beside Newton River, he settled in Orwell and built a log dwelling at the water's edge a hundred yards north of the site of the present Orwell bridge and a grist mill two or three hundred yards farther up the river. The grinding stones came from Pictou, Nova Scotia, for the Island sandstone was too soft for the purpose. This mill was operated by him and later by his son Peter (known as Patrick Steinshole—pronounced Patrick Stya-shell) for several years, and later by Malcolm Gillis (father of Dr. Gamaliel Gillis of Montague Bridge), until abandoned in the seventies. Steinshole returned to Skye in 1804 or 1805, and after marrying Isabella Nicholson, returned with her to the Island on the ship *Rambler* in 1805 or 1806.

Selkirk was able to record in his diary that "The far greater part of the passengers from Skye and Ross have agreed to purchase land—all, in fact, who have property. A few remained who, from poverty, could not. To six or seven families of these I have agreed to make a present of 10 acres each, on the point of Orwell River—good situation for a Village, and have directed that some assistance shall be afforded them in provisions, as well as in furnishing work to them." Hector McDonald purchased 200 acres, and after he paid one-quarter down, "this will leave him about 24 guineas cash to set him up and I think he will do well." Selkirk mentions $1.00 per acre for front lots (i.e., on the sea shore) and half a dollar for back lots. This memorandum gives an indication of the value of the property possessed by some of the settlers. It agrees with the estimate of The Highland Society in its Third Report, wherein it "estimates the average amount which is carried in this way, by the emigrants, at £10 each family of the poorest class, and by some a great deal more: they instance one ship, in which they give reason to suppose that the whole party carried with them £1,500." To people who had never owned land, the prospect of acquiring title to their own homes was thrilling. They were not yet aware of the clamor for free land which later swept the United States and called millions from the depths of misery in Europe to freedom and plenty in that favored land. But they felt the exultant pride of founders who realize they are building a new country with their own hands. Some bought farms at once and became freeholders, whereas leaseholds were not converted into freehold tenure for many years.

We have seen that the log cabins had fireplaces. The iron cook stoves that later gradually replaced these open hearths were objects of a curious prejudice. Food cooked in tightly closed ovens would be ruined, not to mention the danger to health of fumes from the hot metal. Mrs. John Carrier, of Earnscliffe, the former Christina Bruce, of Surrey, Belfast, recalls a story told her by John Robert MacWilliam of Belfast, who was married to her sister. His mother was Sarah Macleod, daughter of "Big Angus," son of Malcolm Macleod, of Glasphein, near Staffin, Skye, who with his wife and family arrived on the *Polly* and settled in Pinette.

"Big Angus" (Angus Mor) was one of the first in the district to buy an iron stove. This he did against the wishes of his father. One night after his parents had retired, Angus had the stove set up in the kitchen. Next morning, when his father entered the room and heard the crackle of burning wood and the roar in the stove pipe, he became alarmed. Waving his arms in excitement, he exclaimed, *"Bristidh e, burstidh e, agus marbhaidh e nah-aile againn."* (It'll break, it'll burst, it'll kill every one of us.) It was not long, however, before iron stoves came into general use for heating and cooking but even as late as the middle of the nineteenth century, recipe books gave instructions for those cooking with open hearths and also for those rich enough to own stoves.

Mrs. Gillis, widow of Malcolm Gillis of Orwell Cove (the former Euphemia Murchison of Point Prim, born February 17, 1847, died March 14, 1942) told the writer in 1939, that when a young girl, her father built a dwelling house without open fireplace, but with an iron cook stove. A few years later, when a member of the family became ill with tuberculosis, the indisposition was attributed to the stove. So suspicious were they of it that the kitchen was enlarged and an open hearth built in it. The same lady, incidentally, recalled cooking barley meal on hot stones on this fireplace; also going to a near neighbor's for live coals when matches were not available. When first introduced, soda was used sparingly, for it, too, bore a questionable reputation. Years later, when kerosene oil lamps were introduced, they also were objects of suspicion. An old man visiting the home of a friend who had one of these lamps watched with concern the new vessel. When the globe cracked, as they frequently did, his only remark was "Without provocation; without provocation." These prejudices are not surprising when one recalls that the potato, long after its introduction into Scotland, was regarded as a vegetable of by no means good character, for it was supposed to influence some of the baser feelings of human nature.

   The pioneers settled along the shore, bays and rivers, for water was their highway in summer, ice in winter. The latter was a constant menace, especially in spring. Horses and men lost their lives breaking through ice worn thin by warm currents or weakened by the sun. Although they rejoiced in the beauty of the forest, it was a constant obstacle to the ambitious who desired fields for grain, roots and fodder but as there was no alternative they threw themselves with enthusiasm into the back-breaking task of turning the forest into arable fields. As proprietors, they felt for the first time in their lives the pride and dignity they instinctively associated with ownership of land. In the homeland, ownership of land was the test of wealth and social position, for the machine age had not yet arrived with its new standards of social values based on the profits of manufacturing, industry and trade.

The most pressing needs were crops of roots, grain and herds of cattle, for these provide the security on which a progressive society depends for advancement. To attain this end, the forest, the great impediment thwarting them on every side, must first be destroyed. In this laborious task the waste was prodigal. During the first few generations birdseye maple and pine trees that today would be almost priceless were destroyed by fire. There still remained the slash and stumps to be disposed of before the land could be broken and tilled. Not till these preliminaries were over could they see the fields of ripening grain that assured, in the words of the Prophet, "plenty of bread" and the security essential for a prosperous and contented society.

Emigration under any circumstances is a hardship not easily endured, especially by women. Only the strong of mind and body can face it. The ties of friendships, locality and climate bind one to the past. Man is as much a part of nature as the inanimate things about him. Only the poor emigrate. The rich and privileged, being satisfied with their lot, remain at home. Colonization with all its grim hardships has thus been left to the hardy poor. Dr. Johnson well understood what emigration meant when he wrote: "To a man of mere animal life, you can urge no argument against going to America, but that it will be some time before he will get the earth to produce. But a man of any intellectual enjoyment will not easily go and immerse himself and his posterity for ages in barbarism."

Because of their numbers, their common language and religion, the Belfast colonists were spared many privations that distress the individual immigrant. Companionship freed them from loneliness, that sore trial of the solitary. A person living in solitude suffers more from lack of human fellowship than from want of the bare necessaries of life.

In the old country the relative social position of servant, tenant, tacksman and chief was governed by rigid rules. On landing in America the emigrant, whatever his social station, had to assume an equal burden and engage in a common struggle against hardship and hunger. The servant was the equal of the master—society became temporarily communistic. The Celtic social system was soon affected by the forces at work around them. People were no longer annoyed by hereditary class privileges and distinctions. They soon recognized no inequality except that of physical strength. There was one class only during the grim period of pioneering. Frugality was imposed on all. No one had anything to spend so no one was disliked for not spending during the dark days of penury in Belfast. Such qualities of birth and breeding as the individual immigrant possessed were not lost in the wilds of their new island home. The hired man lived with the family of his employer on terms of friendship and equality. All dined at the same table and spent the evening together before the open kitchen fireplace. No stigma attached to honest toil in a community where everyone worked with his hands. Unlike the city dweller, who regards certain kinds of work as menial, men and women cheerfully did whatever tasks came to hand. They slaved from dawn to dark, resting from their labor only for church and sleep. There was a feeling of co-operation which did much to make life not only tolerable but actually enjoyable. Simple pleasures they had in abundance, such as fishing, hunting, wandering through the forest and in contemplation of nature. Life was unhurried. The pioneer, delighting in his wild freedom, did what he could and when the day was over did not fret because he could not cut down the whole forest in a year or two. Although anxious to improve their lot in life the acquisition of wealth was not the foremost impulse, for they regarded life here as a mere pilgrimage. Their vision was of eternal life, not of riches.

One should not expect backwoodsmen to possess the social graces of those reared in the city. But despite the lack of cultural advantages the Highlanders were never rough, uncouth people, boorish in speech or manner. Many indeed possessed an innate refinement unexpected in those of rustic appearance. The men were kind to and considerate of their wives and children. Manly and independent they were sparing in praise but extremely sensitive to the censure and reproach of their neighbors. Many sought obscurity rather than risk adverse judgment and reproof. They were quick to anger and although some were strange and quarrelsome, they were equally quick to forgive and forget. They were intensely proud even in their penury. To those in adversity they were compassionate and would share their last bite with those in distress without thought of gain. Their artistic tastes were limited and were expressed largely in flowers and gardens developed by the women. Ships were the delight of men.

The prosperity of a country depends on water and the quality of its soil, as well as on the character of its people. Man pays but little heed to the grass he tramples underfoot, and yet this lowly resource of nature has played a mighty part in the rise and fall of nations. Society has never made any permanent advance where there is a lack of water and where grass does not grow. The most prosperous people are found where the most animals are produced. A shortage of water and grass means fewer domestic animals, less wealth, and a consequent lower standard of living. Belfast has been blessed with good grass and good people.

But the Highlander, and especially the Hebridean, was a bad farmer. The stony soil of the isles from which they came afforded mere patches of arable land. They were thus inexperienced in the type of life they now faced and they and their descendants for three or four generations suffered from their lack of training. Rotation of crops was unheard of and to invigorate the exhausted soil by ploughing down buckwheat or clover was considered a sinful waste. Oats and potatoes were always the most bountiful crops on the Island. The former was sometimes shipped to England. Potatoes were carried to Nova Scotia, Newfoundland and New England in schooners. In 1847 the report of The Royal Agricultural Society refers to the wide prevalence of potato disease. Not until about 1892 did the Colorado beetle appear to menace the crop and harass the grower. Turnips were not grown in quantity until about 1847. As the market was limited and uncertain and means of transport unsatisfactory, there was little to encourage production in a community where man's needs were few. There was thus little call for improved machinery and although the McCormick reaper was being sold in the United States in quantity about 1860 and a mechanical binder was added a few years later, the first seen by the writer was bought jointly by Charles Mackinnon and Allan Shaw, neighbors in Uigg, in or about 1895.

The low market prices that plagued the Island farmer did much to retard a higher standard of well-being. Even at the close of last century oats sold for as low as twenty-two cents, and rarely higher than twenty-five cents a bushel; potatoes for eighteen cents a bushel; eggs for eight cents a dozen; lambs for one dollar seventy-five cents each; fat steers for thirty dollars each. Such prices meant a chronic scarcity of money and a low standard of living. But despite the great economic handicaps oppressing them, these patient, docile people accepted ruinous prices, year after year, under circumstances of discontent that would have driven many other peoples into open mutiny.

It is painful to think that during the history of Belfast, despite steady self-denial and drudgery, no farmer has ever been able to retire and indulge his natural desire for ease on savings from the farm. During and since World War II the produce of the farm has sold for much higher prices and now the farmer enjoys a reward for his labor unknown to his ancestors.

The Hebridean had little understanding of the principles involved in the selective breeding of cattle. Leading the life of lumbermen, woodsmen and shipbuilders, the original settlers and the two or three succeeding generations were not farmers. Tilling the soil was secondary for the first few generations. Improved methods were neglected, and whilst farmers of English, Lowland Scottish and U.E. Loyalist descent in adjoining districts, such as Mutch, Tweedy, Ings, Musick and Carrier, in China Point and Cherry Valley, and Irving, Laird, Enman, Hayden, Vaniderstine and others, in Vernon River, were raising superior stock, they scorned experience and clung to inferior strains of cattle which gave but little milk and less meat. This reluctance to adopt new methods seems strange, for the young people were imaginative and mentally alert and adapted themselves with astonishing ease to the new life. Perhaps the answer is that Islanders have characteristics which are peculiar and different from others. In his travels through Skye, Dr. Johnson remarked that he thought so. "Sir," said he, "when a man retires into an island he is to turn his thoughts entirely to another world. He has done with this."

Every island is a prison
Strongly guarded by the sea.

But though their social and economic progress was slow, advance was being made. It continued steady and unabated, and it is recorded that in the first year after the Selkirk estates were purchased by the government of the Island in 1860, the sum of twenty-five hundred pounds sterling was paid by the tenants on the Selkirk estate.

Nothing shows the steady improvement in conditions in Belfast more clearly than housing. The type and size of house was largely determined by economic conditions. Log houses were in common use until perhaps 1830. When families grew larger better homes were needed.

By this time log was replaced by one and one-half story sawn lumber dwellings. The clipper ship era may be chosen to mark the beginning of the prosperity that warranted still larger and finer homes. In or about 1858 Malcolm Macqueen, of Orwell, replaced the sawn frame structure of five rooms, built about 1827, with a one and one-half story nine room plastered dwelling. This house was occupied until 1896 when a new eight room structure replaced it. Roof and body of these homes were shingled, but strange to say maple flooring though available was not used until late in the century. These houses were drafty, cold and unpretentious. In addition to the kitchen cook stove, there was a heating stove which failed to add much comfort to the bedrooms. All stoves were wood burning. Tables, chairs, cupboards and bedsteads were made by local carpenters. Of silverware and good chinaware there was none. Neither pictures nor ornaments adorned the walls. There were few books.

About 1893 cheese and later butter factories were established by Ontario men at favorable points on the Island. With them began a revolution in farming methods. The quality of cattle was improved and soil impoverished by frequent crops of oats was soon restored to its original fertility.

Pioneering imposes heavy toil on women. In addition to providing clothing for the whole family they assisted at haying and harvest, for these crops were always menaced by heavy rain and winds. In every home the spinning wheel was as conspicuous a part of household furniture as the bedstead, and in many homes there was a loom. Spinning and weaving through long hours, the women beguiled away the time humming or singing well known Scottish ballads, or even psalms—

Verse sweetens toil, however rude the sound;
All at her work the village maiden sings;
Nor, as she turns the giddy wheel around,
Revolves the sad vicissitude of things.

Perhaps no mechanical device ever invented has done more to free women from drudgery than the sewing machine. By 1860 it had become common in the United States but not until about 1900 were there many in Belfast. Installed in factories, they made mass production possible. Cheap clothing followed. Thus was lifted from housekeeping the great burden borne so long and with such patient resignation by the loyal housewife. Thereafter she had some leisure to devote to things she liked better and that were more suited to her aesthetic tastes and physical strength.

For the first century after arrival the settlers were almost entirely free from governmental controls. There was no municipal government on rural Prince Edward Island and so government direction was almost restricted to roads and schools. The first direct tax on land was imposed shortly before 1900. The local school tax was imposed by the trustees. The people took very little interest in politics. Until late in the century the Island was ruled by favorites sent out from England, mostly English of good family with a few Scots and Irish. The people had no power in the matter. Neither their wishes nor interests were consulted. There were no demagogues to incite to dissatisfaction and strife.

By about 1865 the whole countryside for twenty-five miles along the shore from Orwell River to Wood Islands and beyond was occupied by emigrants from the Highlands and Western Isles and their descendants. The pressure of population was then felt. They needed more room for themselves and their beasts, but no longer, as in the past, was there adjacent land available for settlement. Hitherto, lumbering and shipbuilding had provided seasonal employment for the surplus population. But with the gradual decline and final collapse of the shipbuilding boom, this source of employment was at an end. Now there was no work that would afford a decent livelihood for more than one son in a family. The call for labor from the cotton mills and shoe factories of New England, also the building trades, was heard on the Island and the trickle of emigrants that first found their way to Boston and later farther west, soon swelled into a steady stream that never lessened until World War I. There was scarcely a family but had children in the States. Some who attained high position there would have lived and died in obscurity had they stayed at home where the isolation was not over until the narrow gauge railway from Charlottetown to Murray Harbor was opened for traffic in 1906.

This was the period of railway expansion in the States. New lines were built in every direction and especially from the middle states across the Mississippi into the western plains and ultimately to the Pacific coast. The magnitude of these projects brought into existence a demand for products hitherto unknown. The need for housing and public institutions grew beyond the capacity to supply. A boom was underway. Factories sprang up everywhere. People began to flock to the towns where a more prosperous existence could be anticipated than on the farm where life meant unrelieved drudgery. A frenzy of exploration and expansion was sweeping the States. A migrant throng from Europe kept pouring into that Promised Land, some to settle in the cities of the east, others on the great plains of the west where free land and good was still plentiful, the more venturesome to press still farther west into the mountainous El Dorado of silver and gold.

Men from Belfast participated in this vast and stirring movement westward. Moved by the spirit of adventure that won the continent and exulting in the ardor and physical strength of youth, they went forth and pioneered in opening up a world greater and richer than any hitherto discovered in America. Indians were fought, railways built, mines developed, lands broken, rivers bridged, cities built. These hardy pioneers were inspired by the spirit expressed by Gibbon: "The servitude of rivers is the noblest and most important victory which man has obtained over the licentiousness of nature." In the course of two short centuries the stupendous task of subduing a continent was brought to a successful close. Living men could see before their very eyes and wonder at what their forebears had accomplished in that short span of time.

In the States these newcomers soon realized they were in a land of vast resources and unlimited opportunities. They could foresee a future in which poverty and fear of debt would harass them no more.

On visits to their island home young men spoke with enthusiasm of social and political equality; of the fluid social system; of the high standard of living in the States, especially in the cities. These reports opened the eyes of their elders to the backward conditions in the provinces. The older people liked kingship. The pomp of aristocracy appealed to their imagination. But self-interest changes a man's political views, and golden eagles, jingling in the pockets of these young men, was convincing proof of success and had great influence in deciding thousands to forsake their island home and to settle in the nation which had become a symbol of hope for the poor and oppressed of every land. All looked towards the States as towards the promised land.

It would be strange if people who loved freedom were not inspired by the grandeur and success of the American experiment in democracy. In Britain, ancestry was then, as now, more important than achievement. In the States they found a society free from old world prejudices and from many of its restrictions. A man's antecedents counted for little in procuring him a job. The individual was judged by what he could do. Ability to do things well was the test. In the "Old Land" although the laird and common people lived on terms of kindly relations, the tenant had no hope of ever owning land and thereby satisfying the natural longing of all men for independence. They soon realized that in the States they could aspire to wealth and its privileges. Perhaps no factor in the life of this new nation brought greater content to all within its borders than the knowledge that there was equality of opportunity for all.

But potent as were the material reasons for their admiration for American institutions, there were others also that exerted an influence. These people understood democracy. The American theory of government they found congenial, for it was in harmony with the accepted ideals and religious beliefs of the Scottish people. Presbyterianism stood for freedom and for the rights of the middle and lower classes. So did the political theories and practices of the American reformers. The similarity of aim was so obvious and the philosophy of both so alike that many Englishmen called the outbreak in the American Colonies "The Presbyterian Rebellion" instead of "The American Revolution." The leading generals on Washington's staff were Presbyterians, or Congregationalists, as some preferred to call themselves—among them Knox, Sullivan, Stark, Clinton, Montgomery, Mad Anthony Wayne, Morgan and Pickens. John Witherspoon, President of the College of New Jersey, one of the signers of the Declaration of Independence, was Scottish born. At the time of the Revolution, it is estimated that out of a population of less than three million Europeans, over one quarter were of Calvinistic faith being chiefly of Scottish and Ulster-Scottish descent.

As there are no natural resources on the island, except the forest and soil, there is no manufacturing. As a result, the level of material prosperity has been low and people have had to do without many things considered necessary elsewhere. For instance, the farmer, lacking wire and hemp, made rope of grass or straw, called "sugan," for use in protecting his stacks from the gales that lash the coast. A handful of material was hooked over the end teeth of a hand rake, which was then twirled by a man retreating from the person feeding the material to the lengthening cord. Two or three lengths of this rope were thrown across the stack with pieces of fence rail attached to the ends to weigh them down.

The local blacksmith made the iron ice-creepers that were used mostly by old men. They were held to the shank of the shoe by a strap over the instep and, where there was so much glare ice, their sharp teeth along the lower margin prevented many a fall and broken bone. These were probably an American invention, for in the wars between Britain and France, the famous ranger, Colonel Rogers, was expected to construct seven hundred metal ice-creepers to fasten on the shoes of soldiers on the expedition against Ticonderoga and Crown Point, in 1758. Ingenuity was thus developed and many substitutes were made for what they could not afford to buy.

As means of transport were improved and conditions in the outside world became better known, the number emigrating increased greatly, especially after World Wars I and II, when many young people having seen the high standards of living in the industrial centers of Ontario, migrated thither rather than endure the primitive conditions in their native province. The restrictions imposed on immigration into the States after World War I also played a large part in directing emigration from that most favored direction.

During the early years Dr. Angus Macaulay was the medical as well as spiritual adviser of the people. After his death in 1827 there was no college trained physician in Belfast for many years until one Dr. Macneill settled in Vernon River where he practiced until the late eighties.

In 1840, Donald Munro (1819-1884) arrived from Skye, settled in Alberry Plains and for the rest of his life his aid was sought and much of his time spent in aiding others. Roads were never too muddy nor snow too deep to prevent his answering a call. That he helped many is certain, especially in dental extractions, in which he became skilled. He was a likable man and as so often happens in similar cases was attracted to politics. He was elected member of the local legislature for Belfast and was lieutenant-colonel of the third regiment of Militia of Queen's County. His wife was Jessie Robertson (1833-1910) of New Perth, sister of Senator Dr. Robertson, of Montague Bridge. They had several children, one of whom Alice, widow of Clarence Stewart of Little Harbor, N.S. lives, in 1957, in Philadelphia, aged 90. Her sister Margaret, wife of Capt. John Nicholson of Orwell Cove, is survived by two daughters, Jessie and Alice, both in Seattle. The former is wife of her cousin, Leonard M. Campbell, son of Nellie Munro and her husband Hiram Campbell, with one son, Robert. Their brother Lieut. Angus (B.A., U. Sask.) was killed in action in Flanders in World War I.

Marion Munro (1812-1897), sister of Donald, was married in 1842 to Peter Nicholson "Steinshole," miller on Orwell River. Their father, James Munro, had studied medicine in Edinburgh University, in 1785 and 1786, and thereafter until 1840, had practiced in Skye, latterly Uig. In July, 1840, with wife and family he set out for P.E. Island, on the brig *Ruther*, 250 tons, of Sunderland, England. Stricken with pneumonia he disembarked at Tobermory, with wife and two youngest daughters. There he died. The rest of the family sailed on July 27 and arrived in Charlottetown, P.E.I., on Sept. 8, 1840. They spent the winter of 1840-41 in Orwell Cove with Alexander Macleod, a schoolmaster whose wife is believed to have been a relative of Mrs. Munro. He drew wills, deeds and interpreted the statutes for his Gaelic speaking neighbors. His name appears as one of the Trustees in a grant of land from Selkirk's heirs to Belfast Church. Mother and children were reunited in 1841 and late in that year settled on a farm at Alberry Plains near Vernon River.

Each family knew simple herbal remedies and depended largely on hemlock, tansy, dandelion and sarsparilla. Epidemics of smallpox, diphtheria, and scarlet fever occurred frequently, leaving in their wake a memory of fear and sorrow. Tuberculosis caused deaths in almost every home. Even late in the century, when medical graduates practiced in the district, their knowledge of disease was woefully lacking. Antiseptic precautions were neglected, if known. A doctor, after lancing an abscess on a schoolboy's nose, wiped the instrument on his trousers.

For certain slight injuries to the eye they sought and found relief by a method which may have been traditional. To remove lime, which workmen sometimes splashed in their eyes whilst white-washing buildings, or other irritating matter, they used a small concave piece of flint or sea shell which was inserted under the eyelid. One of these shells was in the Macqueen home in Orwell, brought there about 1866 by Peter Macqueen, from Rio de Janeiro, where he had worked for a time as clerk in a bank. It was kept in brown sugar on which some thought it fed. In its course over the eyeball, the shell released irritating foreign matter which was then carried away in the tears. So many were helped by this shell that magic was ascribed to it.

Education

Writers testify to the eager desire for education among all ranks in the Highlands and Islands of

Scotland. Their urge for learning was so fundamental that it seemed to be one of the primary instincts of these people.

Research by the Rev. Donald Mackinnon (D.Litt.) of Kennoway, Fife, formerly of Portree, Skye, and by James Macintyre, of Portree, and other scholars and authorities on Highland history discloses that the people of the Hebrides enjoyed an excellent system of education in the eighteenth century. This was due in no small measure to the fact that the teachers were mature, college-bred men, and usually probationers of the church. Their chief concern was to develop character in the pupil. Some of these dominies were men of inflexible will and gained a lasting influence over many of their pupils. Many of them were among the early migrants to the American colonies. James Madison, a graduate of Princeton University and later fourth President of the United States, attended a school conducted by Donald Robertson, one of these learned Scottish pedagogues. Of him the generous Madison afterwards wrote: "All that I have been in life I owe largely to that man."

With such a background, it is not surprising that a school was opened at once in the little log chapel erected for religious services beside Dr. MacAulay's home, facing and near the mouth of Pinette River.

Two or three teachers emigrated with the settlers. One of them is mentioned by Selkirk in his diary. By way of encouragement, he allowed him a discount of 20 per cent off the price of his land—"Donald Nicholson (schoolm'r) 100 acres 20 per cent advantage."

Schools existed in every parish in Scotland at the time the settlers emigrated. They gave a sound training in the fundamentals of education. The written testimonial, dated November 5, 1811, on behalf of Dr. MacAulay, contains the names of 102 residents. Of these, all but seven who signed by mark, subscribed their own names. This does not mean, however, that all could express their thoughts in writing, for some could not. But it must not be supposed that even these were stupid and uneducated. Incapacity to write correctly implies at most only lack of formal training. Their antecedents, although humble, were good, so that all were likely to inherit intelligence and most did. All could read the Bible in Gaelic and some in English. Many knew it almost by heart. In the new land these people showed that they were moderately endowed and possessed common sense which is more than mere intelligence.

In the wilderness, lack of formal education was no handicap. Physical strength was more essential, and temporarily more prized than learning. Everyone worked with his hands to the limit of his endurance. Leisure was unknown. Physical idleness would be intolerable under existing pioneer conditions. Thus, although learning was always honored for its own sake, formal education had to await more favorable conditions. When every energy is directed to the exhausting task of converting the wilderness into fields of waving corn, the atmosphere is not favorable for formal learning. Pioneers who build a social structure with little more than brawny arms and brave hearts face self-denial and privation for generations. The physical frame is taxed to the utmost to provide food, shelter and raiment, for these demands are inexorable.

An article in the *Guardian* of October 28, 1952, lists schoolmasters who were licensed by the Board of Education up to the end of 1833 as published in the Legislative Assembly journal for the following year. The Belfast region is credited with:

Neil Arbuckle, Belle Creek
Samuel MacLeod, Belfast
Archibald Mackinnon, Point Prim
John MacNeil, Belfast
Patrick Griffin, China Point
Donald Graham, Orwell River
Patrick Doyle, Vernon River
Charles MacEachern, Newtown

Donald MacRae, Belfast
Donald Murchison, Point Prim

And the same newspaper of April 27, 1953, quotes from *The Royal Gazette* of May 20, 1834: "Wanted a schoolmaster of the third or highest class, for the Central District School about to be established at Pinette. Besides the encouragement provided by the act of Assembly for properly qualified teachers of this description (*viz*. £20 out of the Provincial Treasury, exclusive of the sum of £30 at least, to be raised by the inhabitants of the District), the person undertaking the charge of this school will be accommodated with bed, board and washing, free of expense, at the house of the Rev. John McLennan."

John MacNeill, District Schools Visitor, was appointed to this office in 1837. In his first report he condemns the practice of the teacher "receiving his board by going about from house to house, in which case he is regarded both by parents and children, as little better than a common menial." It was noticed, and with dissatisfaction, that those newly arrived from Scotland exhibited evidence of learning much superior to their own, especially in their command of the English language. But if attendance was spasmodic and teaching rudimentary discipline was severe. Playful offences that today would be ignored, were often punished so severely as to border on brutality. For a trivial offence, one of the old masters in Uigg school struck a pupil on the side of the head a blow that rendered him hard-of-hearing for life. These masters enforced discipline. Their authority was upheld by the parents and was unchallenged by the pupil. The rebellious spirit in the classroom today would not be tolerated in those early days.

It might be thought that in the wilderness the young would grow up little better than savages, but such is not the case. Country life deals with fundamentals and ignores the trivial. The sense of perception is quickened and children wandering in the woods and in the open spaces learn to observe the weather, plants, animals and the phenomena of nature in a more intimate way than is possible for city-bred children. Listening to the conversation of their elders around the fireside at night, they learned many things useful to them in later life. Some had great memories and having few books were more diligent in learning by heart than those with the printed word before them. The results of their training showed in helpfulness to neighbors, in respect for women and in care for the aged. An endearing quality was their kindness to birds and dumb animals.

What did these schools teach? In his report to the Board of Education, dated January 28, 1841, Mr. MacNeil states:

The District School of Pinette, under the tuition of the Rev. John McLennan, numbers 30 scholars average attendance. The course of instruction in this school embraces the ordinary and most useful branches of a general English education, in addition to the Latin language. The successful results of Mr. McLennan's laborious avocation are evidenced in the proficiency attained by those children whose attendance has been in any way regular; the pupils of the higher Latin class translate with facility the classics of that language, and display an accurate and extensive knowledge of the construction thereof.

The beneficial effects of the judicious method followed out here of thoroughly grounding the learners in the rudiments of the respective branches is also deserving of notice. Without this, no real proficiency can be attained, and although in the first instance apparently retarding, seldom fails in rendering the subsequent progress of the scholar easy. The reading department particularly has that primary importance assigned to it in this school of which it is deserving, and great pains are taken to make the children acquire a correct pronunciation, tone, and accurate knowledge of orthography, in opposition to the practice of too many instructors of youth, who overlook these details as of minor consideration. The reverend gentleman has now, for upwards of two years, at considerable sacrifice, devoted his time and attention almost gratuitously to the intellectual and moral improvement of the youth of this district of his parish.

We thus see that despite the restrictive effects of poverty progress was being made in educating the young. Mr. MacNeill understood the essentials of sound education. One of the most serious obstacles to higher education for country children was the expense. The nearest seat of higher learning was Charlottetown where the Academy was situated and where the annual fees ranged from thirty to forty pounds, a lot of money for a poor farmer.

Very few families received newspapers or periodicals before 1880. Even letters were rare. Roderick Charles MacLeod of Kinross recalls that the devoted Free Church minister, Rev. Donald Macdonald, Perthshire born, enlightened his congregation by giving a ten minute summary of the news from the pulpit. He was one of the few subscribers to a newspaper in these days.

By about 1850 English books began to appear in many homes. These were reverently preserved but were never in number large enough to warrant the designation library. This indicates a rising standard of living and a taste for reading, for the money paid for a book would buy some much needed article of clothing or household equipment. In the Orwell district of Belfast was organized what was called the Orwell Young Men's Library. It was made up of several hundred volumes. These books were bought by families who kept them available for circulation amongst their neighbors. There were books on history, science, religion, travel and other subjects. They give some idea of the liking of the people for sound literature. In Malcolm Macqueen's home, in Orwell, there were perhaps as many books as in any home in the district. Although the family produced few scholars, they inherited the love of learning that marked their well-known clerical ancestors the Macqueens of Skye and the Macaulays of Skye and Lewis. In this home, where there were two schoolmasters, Peter and Alexander, there were about one hundred volumes, some still extant, among them No. 38, *Sar Obair nam Bard Gaelach*, a collection by John Mackenzie of Gaelic poetry. This volume was a reprint, edited by Norman Macdonald, made in Halifax, N.S., by James Bowes & Sons, in 1863. Well thumbed, it bears the signature Malcolm Macqueen, Nov. 8, 1867. Many a winter evening was spent before the cheerful kitchen fire with family and neighbors who gathered to sing those Gaelic songs that moved the emotions to their very depths. Another work was *History of Rome*, by Goldsmith, bought from James D. Hazard, August 23, 1844; also the *Life of Nelson*, by Southey.

At an early date there was organized in Uigg School a debating club attended by able men such as James H. Fletcher, editor, politician and later lieutenant-governor of South Dakota. At the time the observant Boswell toured the Highlands, he noticed that all classes of any pretensions strove to attain, and in fact did affect an English culture and an English speech. In America, command of English was even more imperative, for it was the sole language of commerce and of opportunity. The Gaels soon perceived that the people with whom they did business scorned their native speech as barbarous, much as in later years their own children, with dual language, looked down, somewhat superciliously it must be admitted, upon those equipped with Gaelic only. Coming from a land where public schools had been in existence for generations and where there was sound learning, they found it hard to bear the sneer of their *Sassenach* neighbors that because they did not speak English fluently, they must be illiterate. Everything, especially their lack of a Gaelic literature, conspired against the use of their native tongue and from the day of landing its use declined. Its fall was so rapid that by 1880 Gaelic was no longer heard in the school and only monthly from the pulpit. By 1900 it had become so unfashionable that it was rarely heard at all. Today only a few aged descendants of the pioneers understand the tongue beloved of their fathers. But long after English became the language in common use, many Gaelic expressions were heard. For instance, instead of herding sheep with the call "sheep, sheep," they used the Gaelic *"kiara, kiara,"* and likewise many other Gaelic expressions. But although Gaelic is now only a memory, English is spoken with an accent and an idiom strongly reminiscent of the Highlands.

We have seen that life in Belfast for the first two or three generations imposed a formidable struggle against the forces of nature. There was no opportunity to rise above mediocrity. The shipbuilder, fisherman and farmer filled important places in the narrow sphere in which they moved, but there was nothing to fire the imagination, nothing to lead to greatness. Education provided the only means whereby they could free themselves from the bondage of insularity and lack of opportunity. The church offered the easiest road to the life the more ambitious sought. The minister with a fluent command of language was admired as much if not more for it than for his learning and piety. Later when the financial position had improved, law and medicine appealed to the ambitious. Although handicapped by a limited English vocabulary, some of the college trained men with an aptitude for languages became "sovereign of words," using English with a precision and exactitude of phrase not always found in the most highly cultivated society. Especially true was this of the Macphail family. But striking personalities were rare and the numbers of those who attained great success in business or achieved renown in any field of human endeavor was not great. What success they had was won by their own effort and not through the merit of others.

On the distaff side, many descendants of these untutored pioneers were endowed with loveliness and charm, and possessed intellectual gifts of a high order.

Not until about 1890 had higher education for women become a matter of public concern. It was still considered unnecessary, although the age-long prejudice against it was diminishing. Women themselves had become conscious of their inferior position and were beginning to demand the removal of inequalities based on sex. They pointed out that women had been Queens and had ruled with distinction. Equality of opportunity in education became one of the first goals in the campaign to emancipate women from their long thraldom. But as the universities made no provision for women students, they were, when finally admitted, treated with condescension. Medical schools in particular were antagonistic. When the fight was finally won, women from Belfast proved by brilliant scholarship and later by professional skill, that they could engage in intellectual pursuits on terms of equality with men.

About 1900, when women physicians were rare everywhere, the Belfast district had the distinction of having at least six in that noble calling:

> Anne Campbell MacRae (sister of Roderick C. MacRae), of Pinette Ponds (M.D. Trinity, Toronto; post-graduate studies in Dublin and Paris). Practiced in Fall River, Mass. Died Charlottetown, 1945.
>
> Anne D. MacRae (daughter of Donald MacRae), Flat River (M.D. Cooper Medical College, San Francisco), Supt. Board of Health Laboratories, San Francisco, died there September 23, 1935.
>
> Ann Young, descendant of Capt. Young of Pinette. Graduate of Medical College, Philadelphia; medical missionary in India for 16 years; latterly, dean of ladies' college in Florida, deceased.
>
> Florence MacRae (M.D. University of

Chicago), daughter of Donald MacRae, Pinette Ponds, master mariner, and his wife, Maud Goodwin; practiced in Chicago.

Florence Macdonald (M.D., University of Toronto; Johns Hopkins University), daughter of John J. Macdonald and his wife, Sarah MacRae (sister of Roderick MacRae, Pinette Ponds), wife of E. P. Pipon, banker, Montreal.

Eliza Margaret Mackenzie (M.D. Dalhousie University), Flat River, served overseas in U.S. forces in First World War. Died at Flat River about 1938.

Isabella Macphail Montgomery (M.D. Tufts), of Orwell.

Mary Mackenzie (M.A. Dalhousie), of Flat River, professor of English at McGill University.

But women with a wide range of knowledge were not confined to University graduates. Many, who for various reasons, but chiefly financial, were unable to pursue formal education, later showed profound knowledge. Among them may be mentioned Isabella Nicholson (daughter of Peter Nicholson, miller of Orwell River, and his wife Marion Munro). Due to an amazing memory, she was known in Belfast as the "Historian." She was wife of John Angus Macqueen (son of Malcolm Macqueen of Orwell, and his wife Margaret Martin of Newtown). Their daughter Matilda Brown Macqueen (wife of Walter D. Ross of Kinross), possesses many of her mother's unusual gifts of mind. If one derives anything from one's progenitors, perhaps no descendant of the Macaulays of Lewis and Skye, and of the clerical Macqueens of the latter isle, inherited more of the intellectual qualities of these families than did the two well-read women, Isabella and Matilda. Despite her years the latter is still a storehouse of family pedigrees and of Skye history, of which she dispenses freely to those seeking her aid.

Among the men who rose from humble station through the medium of higher education a few names that come to mind may be mentioned.

From Pinette came Roderick Campbell McRae, son of Donald McRae and his wife Mary Campbell (daughter of Roderick Campbell and his wife, Anne Morrison, daughter of Neil Morrison, uncle of the famous African explorer, Dr. David Livingstone). After a year or two at Dalhousie University he sailed for Liverpool on the ship *J. H. Myrick*, commanded by his brother, Donald McRae. Entering Glasgow University he won the Thomson prize which entitled him to three years study under the great scientist, William Thomson, later Lord Kelvin. After taking his masters degree from Glasgow University he settled in Chicago, where he spent his business career with

Commonwealth Electric Company. He did valuable work on electric cables and wrote text books on scientific subjects.

The following certificate was given by Sir William Thomson, then Professor of Natural Philosophy in the University of Glasgow:

> The University,
> Glasgow, April 29th, 1882.
>
> Mr. Roderick MacRae, has worked in my Laboratory with but short occasional intermissions, since he joined my classes in November, 1878, and always very thoroughly to my satisfaction. He has shown much ability in making pieces of experimental apparatus, and in carrying out experimental investigations and measurements in various branches of electrical and mechanical science. After his first six months in my Laboratory, he was appointed to one of the Thomson Experimental Scholarships for a year, and has been reappointed for the two following years to the present time, when he leaves to return to his native country. He has proved himself most faithful and persevering in all his work and duties with me, and I have formed altogether a very high opinion of his character; and I believe

him to be well qualified to act teacher of Physical Science.

(sgd.) Wm. Thomson

Alexander Beaumont Nicholson (b. 1845), of Belfast, graduated in Arts from Queens University, Kingston; in 1868 he entered Princeton University, where he graduated in theology. In 1877 he settled in Lansdowne, Ontario. In 1881 he studied in Berlin University and on his return to Canada was appointed lecturer in Latin and Greek at Queen's University, and in 1889, professor. He retired in 1905. His wife Frances Maud Smith was daughter of Francis W. Smith, a brother of Sir Henry Smith, M.P., of Ontario.

Angus MacSwain was born in Belfast, in 1846. After graduating in Arts and Medicine from McGill University he studied in Harvard University and later in Scotland and London where, in 1878, he was admitted Licentiate of the Royal College of Physicians and Surgeons. In 1884 this erudite physician settled in New Westminster, B.C. After a few years he retired to California where he died in 1893. Dr. MacSwain's mother was Flora Nicholson, sister of Hon. James Nicholson, (M.L.A), of Belfast, whose son, Dr. John A. Nicholson, was for years registrar of McGill University. Dr. MacSwain had for partner in

New Westminster, Archibald MacLeod (B.A.; M.D., McGill; New York Polyclinic), who died in New Westminster, October 15, 1884. He was one of six sons of Alexander MacLeod (d. June 14, 1893, aged 70), master mariner, and his wife, Jessie Campbell (died January 18, 1893, aged 70) of Orwell. Dr. Archibald had a brother, Norman MacLeod (b. 1852), whose wife was Mary Ann MacSwain (b. 1852), sister of Dr. MacSwain. One of their children, Floretta MacLeod (b. February 1878), was wife of Dr. Lemuel Robertson (M.A. McGill, LL.D., University of B.C.), formerly of Marshfield, P.E.I., Professor of classics and dean of Arts, in University of B.C. until retirement a few years ago. Their son, Norman Robertson (b. March, 1904; M.A., University of B.C.), Canadian High Commissioner in London, was appointed Canadian Ambassador in Washington in May, 1957.

The said Alex. MacLeod, master mariner, was son of Murdoch MacLeod, of Harris, Scotland, who emigrated to P.E.I. in 1816, and died in Orwell, on May 23, 1860, aged 76. He served in the Battle of Trafalgar. One of the ablest mariners on the Atlantic coast, Capt. MacLeod was asked by Cyrus W. Field, of N.Y. to suggest a suitable terminal in Newfoundland, for the first Atlantic cable.

John Alexander Nicholson was born at Eldon, Belfast, on March 27, 1860, son of Hon. James

Nicholson and his wife Mary Jane Munro, a Newfoundland lady. He graduated from McGill University, B.A. 1887, M.A. 1893, LL.D. 1916. From 1890-1892 he was Superintendent of Education on P.E.I. He was Registrar of McGill from 1902 until retirement in 1930. He died in October 1940. In 1891 he married Catherine Isabel MacLean, daughter of William MacLean, of Point Prim, manager of the Merchants Bank of P.E.I. in Charlottetown. They left two sons, William Cedric Nicholson and James Gordon Nicholson, both lawyers in Montreal, and a daughter Evelyn.

From Flat River came David Wallace Mackenzie. He graduated in Arts and Medicine from Dalhousie University and did post graduate work in Cornell Medical School in New York City. For many years he was a distinguished surgeon in Montreal. He died in 1952 in Charlottetown, aged 77. His wife was Edith, daughter of James St. Clair Moore, merchant, of Eldon, Belfast. Their son, David, graduated in medicine from McGill.

Dr. David W. Mackenzie was son of the late Findlay Mackenzie of Flat River, and his wife, Jessie Cameron, daughter of Ewen Cameron (d. April 28, 1892, aged 95) and his wife Ann Macdonald (d. May 2, 1886, aged 82), who emigrated from Skye, in 1829 and settled in Point Prim. Ewen Cameron's sons, Roderick and Alexander, were outstanding master mariners. Perhaps in the history of Belfast no family was more highly esteemed than the Camerons of Point Prim.

A first cousin of Dr. David Mackenzie, was Malcolm James MacLeod, of Eldon, Belfast, a graduate in Arts of Dalhousie and in Arts and Theology of Princeton University. He was pastor of several leading churches in the U.S., his last being St. Nicholas Reformed on 5th Avenue, New York. His father was Donald A. MacLeod, merchant, Eldon (son of "Big" Angus MacLeod, Glasphein, Pinette), and his wife, the charming Ann Mackenzie, sister of aforesaid Findlay. Christene MacLeod, wife of Donald Macqueen the original settler of the name in Orwell, was sister of said Angus MacLeod.

Among emigrants on the *Dykes* in 1803, were Findlay Macdonald and his wife, Jessie Mackinnon, both from the Isle of Mull, Scotland. They settled in Point Prim. They had six children, among whom was a son, Hector. He married Catherine Maclean daughter of Murdoch Maclean of Point Prim, and his wife, Mary Martin. One of their sons, Alexander Hector Macdonald (b. 1818) was a master mariner. While in command of the barque *Isabel*, of Charlottetown, the ship foundered at sea with the loss of all on board. His wife was Mary McRae of Pinette. One of their daughters, Catherine Macdonald (b. 1846) was wife of Chas. A. Hyndman, of Charlottetown. She lived to be 100. Her son James D. Hyndman, now of Ottawa, was a Justice of the Supreme Court of Alberta. Another son, A. W. Hyndman, was a well known banker, in Charlottetown, where his brother, J. O. Hyndman is an insurance broker. A brother of Catherine's, David Alexander Macdonald (1859-1937), was Chief Justice of the Court of King's Bench, Manitoba, a man beloved by all who knew him. As far as the writer knows he was the first descendant of the Selkirk settlers on Prince Edward Island to become justice of a superior court in Canada. Incidentally, it may be mentioned that Arnold Munro Campbell, a descendant of the Selkirk Settlers of Kildonan, Manitoba, was appointed Justice of the same court, in October, 1947.

Ann, the youngest child of Findlay and his wife Jessie, was wife of Donald Og Murchison of Point Prim. They had ten children. Mary, the eldest, married Angus Maclean of Point Prim. William, the eldest of their nine children was a banker in Charlottetown. He married Flora MacLean of the MacLeans of Portage, Belfast.

Their son Hon. Angus A. MacLean, barrister, Charlottetown, M.P., was solicitor general of Canada. His sister, Catherine Isabel MacLean, was wife of Dr. John A. Nicholson, of McGill University.

Another successful descendant of Findlay Macdonald was John David Macdonald Spence (M.A. University of Toronto), K.C., Chief Counsel of the

C. P. Railway in Toronto.

From Wood Islands came Cyrus MacMillan (1882-1953), (M.A., McGill University, Ph. D., Harvard), Professor of English at McGill, M.P. for Queen's Co., P.E.I. He was son of Hector Colonsay MacMillan of Wood Islands, whose father Malcolm MacMillan, emigrated to P.E.I., in 1806, from Colonsay, Scotland, on the ship *Spencer*. Hector's wife was Isabel Fraser, daughter of Donald Fraser, of Portage, Belfast and his wife Christene MacTavish, emigrants on the *Polly*, in 1803.

The little schools throughout Belfast were of different quality depending largely on the character of the people. For many years Uigg grammar school was considered by many the best in the Belfast area, if not on the whole Island. A group of 84 intelligent and prosperous natives of Skye, mostly from Uig, arrived in Charlottetown, June 1829, on the ship *Mary Kennedy*. They settled on Murray Harbor Road, two or three miles south of Vernon River in the area now known as Uigg, Kinross and Lyndale. In Uig were a few families of MacLeods, Macdonalds, Mackinnons and Gordons, who had seceded from the Presbyterian Church in Skye and become Baptists. Under Rev. Samuel MacLeod as leader they formed a congregation and built a church. These people had a passion for education and the district soon became a "fruitful nursery of talented men" sending forth a steady stream of students to seats of higher learning. Several of the leading lawyers, doctors, clergy, politicians and judges in Charlottetown and elsewhere came from these families. No apology is needed for inserting a few names here. Among them Dr. James MacLeod was the leading physician in Charlottetown for years. Duncan MacLeod was a well known lawyer. Both were sons of Rev. Samuel MacLeod. Malcolm MacLeod, a cousin, was the recognized leader of the bar on the Island for two generations. His cousin Neil MacLeod, was leader of the conservative party and later county court judge in Summerside. His niece Elizabeth McMillan, is now professor in Acadia University, N.S.

John A. Gordon (1847-1933), M.A., Acadia University, studied theology at Newton Seminary, Mass., D.D. He was the son of Peter Gordon, Uigg, and was one of the best known Baptist ministers in Canada. His wife, who was Miss Ford from East Point, P.E.I., died in February 1933, five days prior to the death of her husband, in her 87th year. They had a family of five talented sons. One of them, Alvin H. Gordon, was one of the distinguished physicians in Montreal for many years. Another son, John P. Gordon, merchant in Charlottetown, died January 14th, 1957, aged 83.

Donald Gordon Macdonald (Feb. 15, 1843-Dec. 16, 1931), Vancouver, was a well known Baptist minister. He was son of Donald Macdonald and his wife Margaret, daughter of Donald Gordon, both of Uigg. He married firstly, Margaret, daughter of Roderick MacLeod, of Uigg East, sister of Judge Neil MacLeod, with issue, Minnie, wife of Mr. Avis of Tiverton, Ontario; and secondly, Minnie Schurman, of the famous Schurmans of Bedeque, with issue several children of whom Harold G. Macdonald (Cornell University), contractor, in Edmonton, is one. Minnie Schurman was sister of Jacob Gould Schurman, President of Cornell University and later American Ambassador to Germany.

Donald A. Mackinnon (1863-1928) M.P., barrister, was son of William Mackinnon, Uigg, and his wife, Katherine Nicholson, sister of Angus Nicholson, Orwell Cove. A lawyer, he was Lieutenant-Governor of P.E.I. in the early years of this century. His brother Artemas Mackinnon was a physician in Omaha, Nebraska. Their sister Margaret and her husband George Hammond Brehaut of Guernsey Cove, P.E.I., had five sons, all graduates of Dalhousie University, one, Louis, a Rhodes Scholar. A daughter graduated from McGill.

James Jeremiah MacDonald (b. 1882) son of Archibald J. Macdonald (son of James MacDonald of Uigg) and his wife Marjory Enman of Vernon River, graduated from McGill University; he was chief engineer of Saint John, N.B. Harbor

Commission and of Halifax Harbor Commission and later joined Sir Alexander Gibb and Partners, consulting engineers, London, England, where he died in 1937, leaving a widow and children.

Alexander R. MacLeod, son of Malcolm MacLeod of Uigg (and his wife Esther Robertson, of East Point), son of Rev. Samuel MacLeod, Uigg, graduated in Arts from McGill University; he was a Rhodes Scholar, studied at Oxford University and later was solicitor for C. N. Railway, Vancouver.

Michael Chisholm, from Antigonish, N.S., settled in Uigg in 1832. Later he divided his land with his wife's nephew, Neil Macpherson, a young schoolmaster from Antigonish. His son, Kenneth Macpherson, graduated from Laval University, Quebec City. For many years he was a much beloved parish priest on the Island. His brother, John James Macpherson (M.D., Queen's University), practiced medicine in Castor, Alberta.

Michael Chisholm, a descendant of the original settler of the name in Uigg, was killed in action at Vimy Ridge, Flanders, in World War I.

Donald Cliffe Ross (son of David Ross, of Uigg and his wife Anne Martin of Belle River) graduated in Arts from McGill University, was awarded a Gilchrist Scholarship, studied in Edinburgh University and Heidelberg University; he was an M.A. London University, Osgood Hall, Toronto, practiced law in Toronto. Ross had a prodigious memory and was thought by many to possess the most brilliant intellect ever produced on P.E.I. The Ross family emigrated from Skye in 1821 and settled in the Kinross-Uigg area.

James Campbell Martin, Malcolm Campbell Martin and Samuel Angus Martin were educated in the U.S. where they became Presbyterian ministers. They were sons of Samuel Martin who was born in Skye in 1821, and with his family settled in Uigg in 1829. His wife Sarah Campbell was born in Point Prim in 1829. Another son, John Samuel Martin (b. 1855) was speaker of the local legislature. An elder brother of said Samuel, named Hugh Martin, attended Glasgow University about 1849-51; he became a physician and served in the Confederate Army in Virginia. In that State he married Ella MacCarthy. They left descendants.

James Hayden Fletcher, son of John Fletcher (d. March 13, 1851, aged 38), miller in Uigg, of the Fletchers of Mount Mellick, Pownal, and his wife, Caroline Hayden (d. April 16, 1889, aged 78) of Vernon River, was a remarkable personality. After editing the newspaper, *The Island Argus*, in Charlottetown, for several years, he settled in the western states where he became well known through his lecturing, editorial and political activities. He was Lieutenant-Governor of South Dakota (1889-1891). He died in Gresham,

Oregon in 1910, aged about 80. His brother Pope Fletcher, was a merchant in Charlottetown. Their cousin, Franklin K. Lane, was Secretary of Interior in President Wilson's cabinet. Both families came from Mount Mellick, Queens Co., Ireland.

William Macphail (1800-1852) of Inverarie, Scotland, after spending a couple of years in King's College, Aberdeen, taught school in the Highlands. In 1832 he emigrated to Canada, arriving in Pictou County, Nova Scotia, accompanied by his wife, Mary Macpherson (1804-1888), daughter of a crofter in Badenoch, and their two children. After teaching in Nova Scotia and Cape Breton Island, Mr. Macphail moved his family in 1838 to Belle Creek in the Belfast district, where he taught school; he later moved to Upper Newtown, Belfast, to a farm where he later died. Their son William (1830-1905) began teaching when a mere boy. He was in Uigg Grammar School from 1862 to 1867. In 1864 he bought the Fletcher farm in Uigg. His wife was Catherine Moore Smith (1834-1920), daughter of Findlay Smith, of Newtown. After acting for a few years as school inspector he became bursar of Falconwood Hospital, but retained the farm as permanent home and there their ten children were brought up. The family had an unusual scholastic record, five being university graduates.

John Andrew (1864-1938), B.A., M.D., McGill.

Although he did not adhere to the profession, he practiced medicine in Montreal for a few years. Thereafter, he devoted his life to literature as essayist and literary critic, for which he was knighted. He married Georgina Burland of Montreal. Their daughter Dorothy is wife of Lionel Lindsay (M.D. McGill) of a well known Montreal family. Her brother Jeffrey, a Lieutenant, served overseas in World War I. He passed away a few years ago.

Isabell (b. 1866) graduated in medicine from Tufts Medical College, Boston, Mass.

Janetta Clark (1868-1950), B.A. McGill, teacher.

James Alexander (1869-1947), B.Sc., McGill, professor at Queen's University; Colonel of Engineers, World War I. Married Morage, daughter of Canon MacMorine, Kingston, with son John (M.A., Queen's University), professor, Carleton College, Ottawa.

William Matheson (1872-1942), B.Sc., McGill University. Latterly manager of paving company, Western Canada; married Ethel Penrose, Winnipeg, with issue: Marion, wife of L. M. Delbridge, and Catherine, wife of V. C. Jackson.

John Goodwill (1877-1952), B.A., B.Sc., Queen's University, Director of Marine Services, Ottawa, married Gertrude Georgina Macqueen, New Glasgow, N.S., with issue Andrew and Catherine, the latter the wife of Carl Breuer, Buffalo, of the

U. S. Diplomatic Corps.

Margaret and Catherine Macphail both graduated from Prince of Wales College, the high school in Charlottetown, and taught school. The former was wife of Albert N. Jenkins, of Orwell, with two sons, Ernest and Aubrey, both graduates in science from Queens.

Catherine, wife of Samuel Martin of Heatherdale, has a son, William, also a graduate in science from Queens, who teaches in McGill.

The Church

From remote times the Scottish people insisted on a well educated clergy. The critical Dr. Johnson, who was no lover of Presbyterianism, was astonished on his tour of Skye to find such learning in the clergy. He found them broad of vision and understanding. Such great learning he thought impossible under existing conditions. Referring to Rev. Donald Macqueen, M.A., minister of Kilmuir, Skye, from 1740 to 1785, his travelling companion for several days on Rassay and Skye, he said, "This is a critical man, Sir. There must be great vigor of mind to make him cultivate learning so much, in the Isle of Skye where he might do without it."

In Scotland, university graduates with the master's degree were styled "Maighster" or "Mister."

Although some tacksmen qualified for and used the style "Maighster" as may be seen from Rent Rolls, the clergy, whether graduates or not, were more often honored by this distinctive title. For instance, Rev. Roderick MacLeod would be called Mr. Roderick; Rev. Aeneas Macaulay, Mr. Aneas and the like. Sometimes clergy with the lesser degree, seeking worldly distinction, assumed the title "Sir."

Reflecting on the early church in Scotland Rev. James Murray, M.A., in his *Kilmacolm*, has this to say: "One thing that may strike us as somewhat strange is the title 'Sir' as applied to more than one of these humble priests. These 'Popes Knights' as they come to be scornfully called, were simply priests who had taken only their Bachelor degree. Those who had proceeded to the higher degree were addressed by the more honourable appelation of Maister." Sir David Lyndsay, whose satire did as much perhaps to bring about the Reformation as the preaching of John Knox, thus mocks at what in his day was regarded as an affectation of the priesthood:

> *The pure priest thinkis he gets na richt*
> *Be he nocht stylit like an knicht*
> *And callit schir befoir his name*
> *As Schir Thomas and Schir Williame.*

Presbyterianism has always stood for freedom from absolutist control and for the rights of the middle and lower classes. The Stuart kings and the aristocracy had no liking for it, and for a century attempted to curb its growth and to promote that of Episcopacy. So successful were they that at one period Episcopacy had gained a following so great that Rev. Donald Nicolson, chief of the clan and Episcopal minister of Kilmuir, Skye, was able to report to the Privy Council, in 1666, that there then were only four recusant families in the whole of Skye. But the people found Presbyterianism congenial, and despite ecclesiastical persecution and the opposition of the crown, both long continued, the population of Skye was almost wholly Presbyterian in 1803, and for many years prior thereto. Incidentally, it may be mentioned that in 1929, when in Skye, the present writer was told that there was then only one family in that Island not Protestant, and they were from the mainland.

As the observance of religion was one of the things nearest to the hearts of these pious, credulous pioneers, they were not long in their new homes before they built a church. This was a log structure beside Dr. Macaulay's home facing and near the mouth of Pinette River, on the north side. It was also used for a school. Rev. Dr. Macaulay conducted worship in this log building until 1822, when a clergyman was sent out by the Established

Church in Scotland to minister to these people.

When at length they felt financially able to build a larger church, they chose a site on a commanding height beside the Pinette River. On this situation, fit setting for a Grecian temple, they built in 1824 the modest church in which their descendants worship at the present day.

An article in the Charlottetown *Guardian* of February 8, 1949, gives some interesting details:

St. John's Church, Belfast

Of interest for the information it conveys is the following preamble to "An Act to Incorporate the Minister and Elders of Saint John's Church, in the District of Belfast," passed by the Legislative Assembly in 1832:

'Whereas by a deed of indenture, bearing date the 2nd day of June, in the year of our Lord 1825, Andrew Colville, of Ochiltree and Crommie, in the County of Fife, and of Langley in the County of Kent, Esquire, and Sir James Montgomery, Baronet, Knight of the Shire for the County of Peebles, trustees appointed by the last will and testament of the Right Honourable Thomas Earl of Selkirk, deceased, and the executors thereof, granted and conveyed unto Malcolm Macmillan the younger, of Lot or Township No. 62, Angus Bell, of Lot or Township No. 60, Donald McRae, of Lot or Township No. 58, and Alexander MacLeod, of Lot or Township No. 57, in this Island, farmers, a certain piece and parcel of land in trust for the use of diverse persons of the profession of worship approved by the General Assembly of the Church of Scotland, situated in the Parish of St. John, in the County of Queen's County, containing eight acres, and therein particularly described and set forth; and whereas sundry inhabitants of the District of Belfast, and its vicinity, in the County of Queen's County, being of the Protestant profession of faith approved of by the said General Assembly of the Church of Scotland, have by voluntary contributions erected a handsome building for a place of public worship, which it is intended shall be in connection with the Established Church of Scotland; and whereas it would prove highly advantageous to the said church that the said title to the said parcel of land should be transferred to and vested in the Minister and Elders of the said church, etc.'

The Minister at the time was Rev. John

MacLennan. The builder was Robert Jones, of whom a brief sketch appears hereafter. Mr. Jones kept a day book recording many of his activities. Various and detailed references to the church are found in it, and from them the following extracts are made:

Time spent on sundries for Pinette Church:

1824	First time at Flat River	
	4 days	
	1 day in town	
March	3 days at plans	
	5 days at Flat River	
	1 day in Town	
	1 day in Town	
1824	Received from Hector MacKenzie, Flat River, 18 shillings on account of Drawings for Church	18.0

and under the heading: "Calculations for a Church Pinet Mills March 1824 — 60 ft. long, 42 ft. wide, 19 ft. post" is a list of materials and supplies aggregating about £243. Specifications call for tower with weather cock. Glass and putty to be found by the committee, with all scantling, boards, plank, shingles, etc."

Finally, under the heading: "The Mode of Payment — ½ cash, ½ merchantable produce at the current price going in Charlottetown at the time (that is, as paying a debt to the merchant) ⅓ to be paid after frame is raised, ⅓ when weather boarded and shingled, &c., ⅓ when the whole is finished to the satisfaction of the committee (potatoes not included).

"Tenders to be given in, 8th April.

"The contractor to find two sufficient securities of fifty pounds each."

It is worthy of mention that the original "frow" shingles (hand split, hand planed) may still be seen on the walls of this building.

The artistic inspiration received by Mr. Jones from the Wren churches during his life in London is revealed in the Belfast church. The congregation could not afford much in the way of ornamentation, but the talented builder, at little extra cost, managed to suggest in the spire a touch of beauty which one associates with those London gems of architecture.

The first minister settled in this church was Rev. John MacLennan, who was born in Ross-shire, Scotland, in 1797, and had graduated from Aberdeen University. He was sent to P.E. Island by the Established Church of Scotland in 1822 to minister to his fellow Highlanders on that Island. He returned to Scotland in 1823 and came back to <u>Belfast in 1824</u> with his bride, Catherine McNabb[1].

---

1   *The Scotsburn Congregation* by Rev. Dr. John Murray.

In addition to the great services rendered to his own parish, Mr. MacLennan visited Highland colonies in other parts of the Island. Between 1834 and 1843 he conducted monthly religious services among the Sutherland Highlanders living along Mill River and the South West River; but more than that he went as far afield as Cape Breton Island. In 1827 he made an arduous journey thither and spent six weeks ministering to his co-religionists in that Island. In 1829 he was back again in Cape Breton. On this occasion he visited nearly all the Presbyterian settlements in that colony and baptized two hundred children. In that year, it is said, there were 16,000 Presbyterians of Scottish birth in Cape Breton, although in 1798, when the well known Dr. McGregor of Pictou visited the Island, there were only about twenty Presbyterian families there.

In an age when bigotry was more common than today, Mr. MacLennan maintained a kindly, tolerant attitude to those whose views were different from his own. In the adjoining district of Murray Harbor, he once performed a service which does him credit, although for it he was censured by the Kirk Presbytery of Pictou, on October 12, 1830, in the following words:

"It having come to the knowledge of the Presbytery, that Rev. John McLennan did, this year administer the Sacrament of the Lord's Supper at Murray Harbour, P.E. Island, in connection with a burger minister by the name of Douglas, the Presbytery record their disapprobation of such practices and enjoin Mr. McLennan to avoid acting again in like manner.[1]"

Mr. MacLennan's genial personality, his command of Gaelic and his devoted service on behalf of his people, made him a singularly successful pastor. Equally helpful and beloved was his charming wife. Deeply regretted, he resigned his charge in 1849 and returned to Scotland. While pastor at Kilchrennan, Argyllshire, he passed away in 1852. His family returned to P.E.I. One of his daughters married Rev. Daniel Miner Gordon, of Pictou, N.S., in later years Principal of Queen's University, Kingston, Ontario. Their son, Rev. Dr. Alex M. Gordon, is a well known Presbyterian minister.

By 1861 the population had so increased and economic conditions so improved that a church was built in that year at Orwell Cross Roads for members of Belfast church in that area on land donated by Steinshole. Here the Belfast minister conducted service until 1887 when this branch of the Belfast congregation united with the church on Murray Harbor Road, near Kinross, to form a new congregation. Previous to this the church at Kinross had joined the Presbyterian Church in

1   *The Scotsburn Congregation* by Rev. Dr. John Murray.

Canada. The first minister of this newly formed congregation was Rev. Donald Ban MacLeod (M.A. Park College, Missouri) a native of the district.

After the United Church of Canada was established, the Orwell section joined the former Cherry Valley and Vernon River Methodist congregation to form a new United Church congregation.

The following ministers succeeded Rev. Mr. MacLennan in St. John's Church, Belfast:

> Rev. Alexander Mackay, 1855 to 1859 (M.A., Aberdeen University, 1853). Born, Pictou Co., N.S., 1814; died, 1887.
>
> Rev. Alexander MacLean, 1859 to 1877 (M.A., Aberdeen University, 1853). Born, Pictou Co., N.S., 1822; died there, 1916.
>
> Rev. Alex. Sinclair Stewart, 1879 to 1888 (Queen's University). Born, Tiree, Scotland; died at Montague, P.E.I., 1934.
>
> Rev. Alex. MacLean Sinclair, 1888 to 1906 (Pine Hill Col., St. Fr. X. University). Born, Antigonish, N.S., 1840; died Pictou Co., 1924. Leading Celtic scholar and author, Rev. Donald M. Sinclair (B.A., Dalhousie; PhD., Edinburgh) is a son.
>
> Rev. Samuel D. Macphee, 1906 to 1909 (B.A., Dalhousie University; Pine Hill Col.) Born, Heatherdale, P.E.I., 1865; died Avonmore, Ontario, 1913.

Rev. James W. Mackenzie, 1910 to 1925 (B.A., Dalhousie University; Mont. Pres. Col.) Born Hartsville, P.E.I.; died Charlottetown, 1929.

Rev. Thomas Anderson Rodger, 1928 to 1931, born in Montreal in 1869; died in Winnipeg, November 4, 1950, at the home of his daughter, Mrs. Blair Pitcairn. Ordained in Edmonton, 1904; Presbyterian minister in various parts of Canada. Moderator of Alberta Synod — Chaplain at Vat Cartier camp during World War I. Married Catherine Albert Rymal of Dundas, at Hamilton, in June, 1901. Survived by his widow, one son and three daughters.

Rev. D. Lloyd Griffiths, 1931 (University of Wales). Born in Wales.

Rev. Wallace Wadland, 1937 to August, 1941 (B.A., Toronto University, 1934; Knox Col., 1936). Born in Zorra, Ontario.

Rev. Ernest Charles Evans, supply, Dec. 1941, to Dec. 1947. Born in Litchfield, England, educated in England and United College, Winnipeg. In World War I he served four years overseas in the Canadian Army Medical Corps. Now retired, living in Charlottetown.

R. S. Quigley, 1948 to 1951 (Ph.D., Temple University, Philadelphia). Born in Bothwell, Scotland; died Port Elgin, N.B., Nov. 16, 1951.

Rev. James Heathwood (M.A., Edinburgh University). Born Blackwood, Lanarkshire, Scotland in 1922. Radio Officer Br. Mercantile Marine 1940-1945, Pastor 1952 to March 1955.

The piety and learning of the early ministers won for them a position of power almost equal to that of the civil authority itself. After clerical prestige had declined elsewhere, the clergy on the isolated Island still continued to hold a position of influence.

The church was the center of the social life of the community. All activities on which it frowned were shunned. When the people faced a difficult problem they went to the minister. As worthy ways are learned from good example, the pattern set by the clergy was a vital factor in molding the daily life of the community. The value of sobriety and folly of intemperance were stressed. Their emphasis on obedience to lawful authority was not lost on the people and they maintained a fine record in observance of law and order and a high level of courtesy and respect for others in their daily human relations. It is due to the clergy in no small measure that the stern discipline so characteristic of Scottish home life was maintained for generations in the new land.

Religious service was the great event of the week. People flocked to the church, there to listen with patience to a discourse, often tedious, on points of doctrine. These sermons gave the listeners material for discussion at their daily tasks during the ensuing week. Holding the primitive conception that the Divinity could be moved to intervene directly in the affairs of men, they prayed as if the laws of nature could be manipulated to meet the wishes of the suppliant. In these impromptu prayers, one missed the imposing grandeur that distinguishes the phraseology in the Anglican Book of Common Prayer.

The mystery of life after death was always in their thoughts. Having no knowledge of science to reveal nature, man did not understand his relation to it. Earthquake, electric storm, drought, flood, eclipse and other unusual manifestations of nature were evidence of the wrath of God. They were miracles, not natural occurrences. Inspired by fear, people turned to and received comfort from religion. There was much searching of conscience. Unimportant things were stressed, gaiety and amusements discouraged. Even the most trivial matters were weighed and decided on the basis of moral consequences to the individual. There was a marked difference between the grim religion of the Scot and the tolerant belief of the English.

The form of religious service was simple and austere, as befits a democratic institution. The whole congregation stood during prayer and sat while singing. In the Methodist church, in adjoining Vernon River, the congregation stood while singing. During prayer in that church many dropped on their knees, backs to the pulpit. The young Presbyterian visitor, unacquainted with and sensitive to any show of religious fervor by the audience, was startled by the loud "Amens" that arose from enthusiastic worshippers throughout the audience.

Saints' days and church festivals had long since been abolished, leaving Sunday the only church day in the year. Funeral, marriage, and christening ceremonies were usually held in the home. In remote districts where a minister was not available to baptize Protestant children, the kindly Roman Catholic Bishop MacEachern, on his visitations was sometimes requested to perform that function. This service was deeply appreciated by the family honored by the distinguished prelate's visit.

The Sacrament was the most solemn function in the church year. In the early days it was held once each year. Later it was held twice and even oftener. It was conducted in the manner customary in all rural Presbyterian churches. Preparatory services in Gaelic and English were held on the three days preceding Sacramental Sunday and a final service on Monday. An atmosphere of solemnity pervaded the community during this season.

The Bible was an object of veneration. When, through frequent use it was worn almost to tatters, many feared to burn it, dreading dire calamity. Rather than tempt Providence by an act of seeming impiety, they buried it in the ground.

Rural communities are notorious for primitive religious ideas, prejudices and hatred of change. Belfast was no exception. In no particular were these characteristics more noticeable than in their observance of Sabbath. The most harmless pastimes were forbidden on that dismal day, not to mention labor advantageous to the community. Even when a downpour threatened, as it so often did in that fickle climate, the farmer refused to gather his precious grain on Sunday, even though its loss meant serious privation for the ensuing year. As the traditional habits and institutions of an old civilization cannot be changed or effaced in a day, it was a century before the settlement began to emerge from the unreasonably strict standards of preceding generations. The questioning spirit of science had finally arrived and with it almost the last trace of sectarianism and church discipline disappeared.

Many representatives of the Highland clans assembled in Belfast Church on August 5, 1951. Interest was added by the presence of Dame Flora, Mrs. MacLeod of MacLeod, Dunvegan

Castle, Skye, Chief of Clan MacLeod, who with her daughter, Mrs. J. Wolrige-Gordon and twin grandsons, John Wolrige-Gordon and Patrick Wolrige-Gordon, were then on the Island. As reported in the *Guardian* the following day, she found the place "a beautiful spot where rest a very large number of Highlanders, a great number of whom came from Skye, many bearing the name MacLeod."

During the same week Belfast was visited by the distinguished Highland historian, Rev. Dr. Donald Mackinnon, of Kennoway, Fife and his daughter, Miss Mairi K. Mackinnon (M.A., Edinburgh University). Dr. Mackinnon spent two weeks on the Island assisting Rev. Mr. Bishop at services in the Free Churches there, having been sent by the Free Church in Scotland to visit congregations of their persuasion in the larger cities in Canada.

Mills

From earliest times the mill played an important part in the life of rural communities. The miller was a man of influence. They were skilled artisans, and despite many jests to the contrary were, with few exceptions, men of integrity. As the mill often descended for generations from father to son, family tradition and family pride, both valuable assets in business and social relations, developed through the years and many families of millers played a vital part in adding to the wealth and happiness of the communities in which they lived. There was thus built up a fine tradition and we are the losers that so many of these notable old families, for various reasons but chiefly economic, have been forced to abandon this ancient and honorable calling.

But the poor miller had much to endure. He took toll for his work and as he was often the object of envy, he was frequently accused of taking more than his fair share. For grinding wheat, rye, barley, oats, buckwheat or Indian corn, millers were limited to a maximum toll of one-sixth part of the product, according to an act of the legislative assembly passed in 1834 and reenacted with amendments four years later. Some indeed took more than the law allowed. If there was no cause for complaint on this score many found one anyway. One family found the flour too coarse; another found it too fine; grit from the stones got into the flour, as it certainly often did, and from it between the teeth. Finally, they went to a neighboring mill, only to return again to their former choice in a few months. Despite all the criticism levelled at them the millers were worthy citizens and rendered a service to the community that was quite indispensable, even if not fully appreciated by all at the time.

Throughout the Island there was a mill or two on every stream. On the Orwell River, Steinshole built a grist mill at an early date. In 1829 or earlier George Gay from Lot 49, built a saw mill, later operated by his son John, who bought the adjoining farm and later sold it to John Fletcher, who built a grist mill farther up the stream. This mill was later sold to John F. MacLeod, of Strathalbyn, who operated it until early in the 20th century. The farm was bought in 1864 by William Macphail, the schoolmaster in Uigg. There has been no mill on this river since the MacLeod mill was abandoned. Remembrance presents a picture of happy rural life around these mills. There was the kindly miller, who kept a rod and line for those who wished to fish for trout while waiting for their grist. Such as preferred to shoot beguiled away an hour behind an alder awaiting the ducks which sometimes swept down on the pond, where in winter the children gathered to skate. Then there were the wonders of the mill; in the older mills, the giant wheel over which the water fell to the foaming pool that concealed in its mysterious depths delectable trout; the noisy clamor of the grist mill, the strident whine of the circular saw cutting through the knotty log, and above all the tremor that presaged the early collapse of the whole structure into the stream.

The earliest of these mills was on Pinette River near Belfast church. Lord Selkirk consulted James Lewis Hayden, the skilled millwright of Vernon River, in 1803, about a new mill he proposed to build on the Pinette. It was probably built in 1804 or 1805, for Selkirk. William Johnston, writing Selkirk from Charlottetown on December 29, 1815, mentions that Jones and Patton are in the saw mill at Pinette and that they are "behind the rent, altho' Jones is an industrious laborious man." He mentions the "repeated breaking down of the dam which had been faulty in its original construction, and they have also been at considerable expense in repairing and rebuilding the saw mill and in erecting the Grist Mill."

Robert Jones, who is referred to elsewhere as builder of Belfast Church, was, with Mr. Patton, tenant of this mill in 1815 and 1816, and perhaps earlier. Mr. Jones was a methodical man. With meticulous care and exactitude he kept a daily record of the work on which he was engaged. Sketches of machinery and of buildings, in his fine clear hand, show the exact and artistic nature of the man. From this diary, now in possession of his great-grandchildren, Locke Jones and sisters, Misses Sarah and Maude Jones of Pownal, the following lines have been extracted:

Repairing Pinet Mill Dam
15 Sept. 1815

	Jones, McDougall & McWilliams	1 day each	3
20th	Jones & McDougall }		
	Finlay Smith }		
	Donald Smith }		
	Charles McKinnon }	1 day each	8
	Andrew Smith }		
	Allen McDougall }		
	John McTavish }		

and so on —
and

Mill Account

1815	August 9	Anderson	2 Wheat
	August 30	Holiday	2 Wheat
	September 1	D. Ross	1 Wheat
1816	Apr. 5	Angus Fraser	1 Wheat
	Apr. 8	John Nicholson, Orwell	1 Wheat
	Apr. 16	Mrs. Williams	1 barley
	Apr. 19	Alex. McDonald	1 F.B.

Alexander Maclean of Portage, Belfast, writing to Andrew Colville, Esq., London, England, agent for the Selkirk estate on P.E. Island, under date 7 February, A.D. 1839, among other things said, "a few weeks ago the grist mill at Pinette was totally consumed by fire." He further asserts "that the mills have been unprofitable to his Lordship ever since built thirty-five years ago. Every tenant left them worse than when he came and paid a mere fraction of rent and plundered the pine lumber on it." Here follows a list of tenants:

Spraggens
Jones and Patton Macpherson
Morrison and Hayden Morrison alone
Gill Curtis

And: "It can easily be ascertained that these all put together scarcely paid three years rent, exclusive of stumpage, for the immense quantity of pine which they destroyed on the property. There are now no buildings on the property worth mentioning except an old saw mill and a kiln built last summer, now about half finished. Besides the dam has fallen in two places, and will cost considerable to repair."

Mr. Maclean ends by offering "£250 Halifax currency for the premises as they stand and the fifty acres adjoining the mills, payment to be made next summer if it meets your and Mr. Cunard's concurrence."

Mr. Maclean's offer was apparently rejected, for soon thereafter Alexander Dixon (b. 1819, d. 1880) a miller of Bowport, Northumberland, England, who had migrated to the Island in 1832 and settled near Mount Stewart, bought the property and operated a carding, grist, and saw mill. His parents were Alexander Dixon, miller of Bowport, and his wife, whose maiden name was Carr. Alexander, first of the family in Belfast, married Margaret, daughter of Colonel Milbourne of Berwick-on-Tweed, Scotland, an officer in the British Army. The mill was operated by this fine family from that day until about twenty years ago, when it was sold to Daniel Macpherson, of Bellevue, who operates the saw mill today.

Alexander Dixon, son of Alexander Dixon 1st in Belfast, married Jessie, daughter of the aforesaid Alexander Maclean. She lived until her death a few years ago at 95, with her daughter Margaret Milbourne (widow of Roderick E. Macdonald) and her two brothers, Maclean Dixon and Joseph Dixon.

The late Angus A. MacLean (1855-1943), former member of parliament, and solicitor-general of Canada (son of Jessie's sister Flora and her husband William MacLean of Point Prim, later private banker of Charlottetown), recalled an incident of his boyhood days in Belfast which reveals the ready command of the Bible that distinguished these early pioneers.

At noon on a sunny day in spring, he and two

or three companions wandered along the Pinette, then swollen by spring freshets. They were remarking on the danger to the mill when Mrs. Dixon was seen crossing the dam. Soon a loud crashing noise warned them that it had broken away. In an instant a wall of rushing water swept dam, ice, logs and everything movable in its path down stream. In the midst of the moving mass of wreckage Mrs. Dixon could be seen bravely struggling for life. Her husband, who was a spectator of this unusual scene, rushed to the bank shouting words of encouragement to his endangered wife. "Poo Margaret! Poo Margaret!" he would cry in his Old Country dialect as he ran along the bank trying to overtake her. Finally, when the mad rush of "mighty waters" had partly subsided, he helped her to safety, exclaiming with half-humorous concern in his excitement as he dragged her ashore, "When thou passest through the waters, I will be with thee; and through the rivers, they shall not overflow thee." (Isaiah:43-2)

Until grist mills were built in the Belfast area farmers brought their grist in row-boats to mills in Millview or the Pownal district.

The *Guardian* of September 21, 1949, reproduced the following account of an earlier disaster to the Pinette Mill dam from the pages of the *Colonial Herald* of November 30, 1839:

There are few of our readers who have not seen or heard of the Pinette Mills. Whoever has travelled that road must have been struck, on the sudden turn which takes place in the road, when the church and parsonage house suddenly burst on the view, and advancing still further, he finds the vale traversed by the placid stream of the Pinette. Between the crest of the acclivity which we speak of, and the church, are situated the Pinette Mills, about a hundred yards above where the bridge crosses the stream. A new grist mill and kiln have lately been erected by William Douse, Esq., agent for the Earl of Selkirk, which, in point of workmanship, are second to none in the Island.

On Monday last, the dam, eighteen feet in height, gave way with a sudden crash, which alarmed the whole neighborhood. The materials of which it was composed were hurried down the stream with a velocity surpassing description, and how the bridge came to resist the shock can hardly be accounted for. The deprivation of such a useful mill was a calamity of no ordinary character; but we are happy to say, that the whole population, with a unanimity which does them credit, at once hurried out and were all busily engaged in repairing the damage, so that in a short time we may expect to hear that the mill will be in full operation.

In the days when forests covered the land precipitation seeped through the sandy soil to reappear as bubbling springs. These springs were a delightful feature of the countryside. There were several on every farm and were used instead of wells. Throughout the year they poured a constant stream of pure water into the rivers. But when the forest was destroyed and the land brought under cultivation, the blanket of snow that, shielded by the forest had formerly taken months to melt, now dissolved quickly and like the rain, rushed down the slopes into the rivers.The eroded soil carried in these sudden freshets filled up the trout pools that had been so attractive a feature of these gurgling streams. As the soil was thus deprived of a reserve of water, most of these streams dried up and rivers that once were constant in volume and of considerable depth throughout the year are now a mere fraction of their former size, except for a few days in spring when, increased by flash floods, they become raging torrents.

Lumbering

Even a few years before 1800 Nova Scotia and New Brunswick had been exporting increasing quantities of logs to England for masts. Napoleon's efforts to cripple England by cutting off her supply of timber from the Baltic gave great impetus to the industry in British North America. Down the rivers were floated vast rafts of logs and squared timber bound for the seaports for shipment to England. The rivers Saint John and Miramichi became famous. The valley of the latter probably produced more timber than any other region of equal area on earth. In Quebec the trade was spectacular, for the vast forest wealth of the Ottawa and St. Lawrence valleys poured into it as common center for shipment to England. The industry deeply affected the economic life of the people. Lumber camps provided a ready market for products raised on the farm. Young men secured seasonal jobs that helped establish them in their new homes. The profits won in the timber and shipbuilding trades helped provide the capital needed in opening up the new country. Ships returning in ballast provided cheap passage and thereby greatly encouraged immigration from the British Isles. When a tree was felled, an axeman scored it where it lay. The wood between the scores was then beaten off with a small axe by the "rough" workmen. It was then faced by the skilled broadaxemen. The skill of these lumbermen cannot but arouse our admiration. Some became so expert that they could square a log without using a blackline. The surface showed no trace of the score, being as smooth as if planed. This unsawn timber was sold by the ton and was known to the trade as square-timber or ton-timber. It was not dressed to a proud edge, as handling would then have chipped and splintered the edge. To avoid this danger the ends were chamfered. The English buyers preferred nicely dressed timber and paid better prices for it. Once dressed, the timber was hauled on sleighs by oxen or horses to the shore, whence it was rafted to a port for shipment to England.

Hunting

When the pioneers arrived on this continent they found a land teeming with wildlife. Early settlers recalled that for many years after their arrival flocks of ducks and Canada geese in countless thousands darkened the waters of the rivers, bays and harbors as in spring and fall they migrated along the coast. Into these waters they swarmed in search of food, fresh water, and shelter from the storm. Geese made night melodious with their honking. As these magnificent birds took the air in early morning, they produced by the flapping of their wings a noise like the roar of distant thunder. The clamor of their calling was a summons to the hunter to shoulder the long muzzle-loader hanging over the kitchen fireplace. Many fell to the hunter's gun on points over which they flew in passing to and from the open sea. Hunting was a passion with many. Prowess with the gun was a source of family pride and frequent conversation

Curlews, yellowlegs and other waders covered the mud flats. Upland plover wheeled over the hay meadows in such vast numbers that a single discharge of a gun brought down a dozen or more at a time.

Today such stirring scenes live in memory only. As the settlement of the continent proceeded, the face of the country became completely changed. Forests were cut down, swamps drained, the land plowed. Deprived of the seclusion and protection essential to breeding haunts and pursued by an ever increasing number of hunters armed with modern firearms, many species have vanished completely, whilst of others there remain a few sorry specimens only.

Fishing

Fish was the main diet for generations. The waters abounded with many varieties. Some could be taken at all seasons of the year; others advanced along the coast at regular intervals. Herring were so plentiful that a haul of a net supplied a family for months. Cod and herring were the staple diet for generations. Lobsters were abundant. Brook trout and the delectable sea trout provided sport on every stream. Trout, lobster and mackerel were the prime table delicacy. When the taste became sated with the diet of fish one could pick up on the shore more clams and oysters than could be used. Deep beds of oyster shells are still found in Orwell River and in many other rivers, bays and harbors. In winter the farmers dredge through the ice and carry these shells to their fields to fertilize the soil. Hillsborough Bay was a fishing ground well stocked with cod and herring till about 1865 when for some unaccountable reason they ceased to haunt its waters. It was customary for groups of young men to go in open boats to these grounds to procure a supply for the ensuing year. St. Peter's Island, only ten or twelve miles distant, was a favorite camping ground. Here they occupied temporary huts and fished for three or four weeks each summer. After the family needs were provided the surplus catch was sold to American fishermen for bait for deep sea fishing.

These short summer expeditions made up of groups of eight or ten neighbors appealed to the young men, for it was an agreeable diversion from the monotony of farm life. It was a valuable experience, for it trained them not only in the art of seamanship but to observe the variations in the weather. In an age when there were neither aids to navigation nor weather forecasts, it was very important even for farmers to be able to interpret the message of the sun dog, northern lights, clouds and the various other more subtle manifestations of nature. To be forewarned of an approaching storm was to guard against it and thereby to save property and in some cases even life itself.

Although mackerel were less important than cod or herring as a source of food, their arrival on the coast aroused much greater enthusiasm for they provided diversion from the dreary monotony of farm life. Fishing then was sport, not work. No sooner was it known that they had arrived than word was passed around. Boats were manned and rowed or sailed to wherever the fish were seen. Mackerel are surface feeders and on a sunny day their presence is revealed by a ripple on the water. When the boat drew near the school, fistfuls of ground herring were scattered on the water to attract the fish. A hook baited with red flannel was cast overboard and the silvery fish hauled in as fast as a man could work his arms. Haste was necessary for mackerel are fickle and stop biting without apparent cause. Taken ashore the fish were split, dressed and put in pickle for table use.

Ships and Seafaring

"Behold also the ships, which though they be so great and are driven of fierce winds, yet are they turned about with a very small helm, whithersoever the governor listeth." James: 3-4.

The building of wooden ships was closely allied with the lumber industry and for a time was almost as important. Owing to the urgent need for dwellings and cleared land, the settlers were compelled for a few years to ignore the call of the sea and to content themselves with building small boats for coasting and fishing.

As they gained experience, larger vessels were built, and soon local schooners were used to carry produce to Nova Scotia and Newfoundland. The first Belfaster to trade with Nova Scotia seems to have been Hector Mackenzie of Flat River, who owned a schooner. Donald Nicholson, the miller on Orwell River, also traded with Nova Scotia and Newfoundland.

An interesting reference to the trade with Newfoundland, in 1803, was made by Selkirk, who records that this colony provides the chief market for the produce of the Island, particularly of well fed beef. Of tonnage, "it is computed that about

70 vessels belong to the Island, the greatest part schooners of 30 or 40 tons — some larger — but only one or two brigs or vessels of size ..." From a very modest beginning, the industry grew from year to year until about 1840, when the era of clipper ships began; there were shipyards on every navigable river and harbor in the land. Around these yards, knees, logs, and timber were piled high. Between 1865 and 1870 the industry had reached its peak, and thereafter, unable to compete with steam and iron, and fell into decay. It is recorded that between 1830 and 1873 there were 3,000 vessels averaging 200 tons each built on P.E.I.

Many ships were built on commission for British shipping firms, for building was cheaper in the colonies than in Britain. All found a ready market, for they were in great demand for carrying passengers from Britain to Australia and the United States, and on their return voyage cargoes of wool from Australia and cotton from the Southern States. The material profits from the industry were great, and added much to the general prosperity of the colony.

The largest shipyard in the Belfast district was at the confluence of the rivers Vernon and Orwell. It was operated by Benjamin Davies of Charlottetown, eldest son of Nathan Davies, who was born in Pembrokeshire, South Wales, and who, in 1807, emigrated to the Island as a boy of twenty. Farther up the Vernon was a yard operated by William Welsh, master mariner, also a native of Charlottetown. Incidentally, it may be mentioned that Louis H. Davies (son of Benjamin) and Mr. Welsh represented this riding in the House of Commons for many years. For a time Mr. Davies was Minister of Marine and Fisheries. Later, as Sir Louis H. Davies, he served as Chief Justice of Canada.

These two yards built many ships, but they rarely exceeded 250 tons. The last vessel built on the Vernon was launched in 1867 below the Hayden shipyard and near the headwaters of the river. She was called *Natalie*, and was built and owned by Thomas Richards, whose family is still represented in the district. Sixty men were employed in this yard.

In these local shipyards the practice was to lay the keel in March. Sometimes sixty or seventy men worked on the ship and in the yard. At sunrise the men were hard at work. The yard hummed with the ring of hammer and the sound of saw. Breakfast was not served until eight o'clock. The day ended at sunset, and for that long period of toil the wage in the early days was only forty cents, and part of that in trade. Those selling logs were paid part in cash, part in merchandise, usually tobacco, wheat flour, raw sugar and other supplies carried in the yard store. Watson Huntley of Vernon River, who died in 1945, aged 86, recalled that his father, Henry Huntley, son of William Huntley, a shipbuilder emigrant from Bristol, England, was paid from $1.00 to $1.10 per day for cabin finishing, half cash, half merchandise. The most intelligent men in the community were attracted to these yards, for originality was encouraged. Sound materials and honest construction were essential. The beauty of line, the speed, the seaworthiness of these ships is a lasting monument to the ingenuity and integrity of these designers and builders. They were masters of their craft. Although incapable of laying down on paper a working plan of a ship, their knowledge was so complete and accurate that the product of their head and hand was a thing of strength and beauty. Nor was the artistic side neglected, as is proven by the delicate paneling in the cabins. This work exhibits the artistic taste and manual skill of the ships' joiners of that age. Into these ships the workmen put something more than the labor of their hands. They knew the very trees that went into yards, masts, ribs and plank. So when the craft was finished they attributed to it something of their own personality. Individual ships won their devoted loyalty. Their relative merits were a constant topic of discussion; their careers were watched with an anxiety usually reserved for human beings. Many a ship sailed away manned from cabin-boy to master by a crew known to each other all their lives, and in many cases, near relations.

The ships were finished in the fall in time to sail before freeze-up. Oats, potatoes, timber and other products formed the cargo. Ships in the West Indies trade often carried horses. On the return voyage they brought back cargoes of sugar, molasses, tobacco, rum, salt, and other tropical products.

From the moment the ship cast off her moorings and started on her voyage, the sailor had experiences that tested his strength, courage and endurance to the uttermost. After everything was ship-shape, late in the afternoon on the day of sailing, the mate, second mate, or boatswain called all hands aft to pick the watches. The mate first chose a man and ordered him to stand on the port side of the deck. The second mate then chose one and ordered him to the starboard side. Alternate choices were thus made until the whole crew was divided between the port—the mate's watch, and the starboard—the second mate's watch.

As soon as the watches were picked the mate generally addressed the assembled men somewhat after this fashion: "Men, we are now bound for China. You'll find the ship a good one if you behave and do your work. If called at night to shorten sail, get out quick. If you act like men you'll be treated like men." A mate once concluded his brief address with the pithy comment: "When I walk, you run; when I run, you fly."

The mate next gave an order in the following or similar words: "Port watch go below and get supper, and when supper is over come on deck and relieve the starboard watch to get supper."

During the days of sail the more romantic and adventuresome boys found an outlet for their energy at sea. They made brave, loyal and skilful seamen. Travel gave them new ideas. It was not uncommon for boys of fourteen and even younger to take their place in the forecastle. Some were anxious to improve their minds, and after a few years passed to the cabin. The master mariner was a man of standing in his community. Travel and experience widened his range of knowledge and when his career at sea was over he was a well educated urbane gentleman, often of means. Many returned to the old parish to spend their declining years on or near the homestead on which they were born. The sea exacted a heavy toll and there was many a sad home. In Point Prim nearly every family lost one or more members. Some were drowned, others were victims of accident or disease. Perhaps no family in the district suffered more than that of John Murchison. His headstone in Mount Buchanan burying ground, Point Prim, bears the following inscription:

John Murchison
d. Oct. 16, 1904, aet. 83
His Wife Isabella Macdonald
d. May 12, 1911, aet. 83

Isabella Macdonald was aunt of Chief Justice Daniel Alexander Macdonald of Winnipeg. And in the same plot stands a stone inscribed as follows:

In Memory Of
Capt. Hector, d. of yellow fever, at
Bolivar, South America, July 20, 1881,
31 years, 8 months.
Also Neil, Seaman, d. of smallpox at
Liverpool, G.B. March 23, 1871, aged 19.
Capt. Angus, drowned at Newfoundland,
Dec. 81, 1890, aet. 33.
Also Alexander, 1st mate, drowned in New-
foundland, Dec. 31, 1890,
aged 23 years and 8 months.
Also Donald, quartermaster, drowned in
Bay of Biscay, Mar. 20, 1869, aet. 21.
Mary Ann, d. Jan. 14, 1866, aet. 7 days.

The large part seafaring played in the life of Belfast up to about 1900 may be judged from the number of master mariners from that district. These men made a great contribution to the arts of navigation. The following list (except for a few names since added) appeared in the *Charlottetown Patriot* of April 22, 1922.

From Point Prim:

Murchison	Hector M.	Lost with all hands, including 12-year-old son, on *Atlas* liner. New York to Cuba.
	Neil M.	Died in Vancouver.
	Murdoch M.	Lost with all hands, including brother John, 2nd officer, barque *Assyrian*. New York to London.
	Hector J.	d. Yellow fever. Venezuela.
	John J.	d. Charlottetown, 1925.
	Angus J.	Lost (aged 33) with all hands on brig *Tanta* on Newfoundland coast, Dec. 31, 1890, also his brother Alexander (aged 23), first mate.
	Malcolm	d. North River.
	James	Lost with all hands, brig *Helen Davis*. Charlottetown to Barbadoes.
	John James	Buenos Aires (son of James).
	Peter	d. Charlottetown.
	Roderick	d. San Francisco.
	Neil D.	d. 1946. San Rafael. Calif.
	Peter D.	d. San Francisco.
	Donald D.	Killed in 1929 in fall in hold of ship in Seattle.

Macdonald	Alex. Hector	Lost with all hands, ship *Isabella*.
	Samuel Roderick	d. Charlottetown.
	Murdoch R.	Drowned. Halifax.
	John D.	Pinette.
Finlayson	William	Lost overboard on voyage to Africa.
	Kenneth	d. Charlottetown.
MacLean	Samuel	
Cameron	Roderick	d. Charlottetown.
	Alex.	d. Charlottetown (brothers).
MacLeod	Donald M.	d. Point Prim.
	Alex.	d. Point Prim.
	Malcolm	d. Winnipeg.
MacRae	Murdoch	d. New Zealand.
	Martin	Lost with all hands, including his wife Catherine Ross, Flat River, on U.S. ship *Samaria*, off California coast.
	John	Lost with ship *Anglo-Indian* (part crew saved) on Formosa Island.
	Alex.	Accidentally killed in San Francisco.
	Donald A.	d. Point Prim.
	Murdoch D.	d. Point Prim.
	Donald	d. Annandale, P.E.I.
Nicholson	Samuel	Lost overboard, steamship, off Sandy Hook.

	Malcolm	Master when ship *Simla* run down, English Channel. (All saved.)
Gillis	John	d. Glasgow.
	John	Born, Skye. d. Charlottetown, 1931, aged 99.
Buchanan	Samuel	Breadalbane, P.E.I.
Lockman	Peter	Lost with all hands except cabin boy, near Madagascar.
	Malcolm	d. Bermuda. Supt. Quebec SS. Co., N.Y.
Macaulay	Allen	d. at sea, near San Francisco.
	Alex.	d. near Portland, Maine.
MacIver	Donald	

The youngest master was Samuel MacDonald, who at 18 commanded the brig *Tam O'Shanter*, owned by Daniel Davies, Charlottetown.

Master Mariners from other parts of Belfast:

MacLeod	Roderick (Ho ro)	Orwell Cove. d. New Zealand.
	Donald	Orwell Cove, d. smallpox. Liverpool.
	Alex. Wm.	Orwell Cove, d. Charlottetown.
	John, Sr.	Orwell Cove, d. Orwell Cove.
	John, Jr.	Orwell Cove, d. N.Y., 1934.

The above five were brothers, sons of Wm., son of Roderick MacLeod, "Ho ro" first of Orwell Cove. "Ho ro" was a form of salutation or greeting perhaps, as in the Hebridean song: *Ho ro mo nighean donn bhoidneach*—In English, "Ho ro, my nut brown maiden." To distinguish various branches of this MacLeod family from others of similar Christian name they were designated "Ho ro," for example "Roderick Ho ro," "Alexander Ho ro," etc.

MacLeod	Murdoch "Beag"	Orwell Cove, drowned in Pacific.
	Alex. Sr.	Orwell, d. Orwell, S.S. *Gulnare*.
	Alex. Jr. (a son)	Orwell. Drowned Quebec, S.S. *Gulnare*.
	John	Orwell, d. sailing out of New York.
	Neil	Orwell Bridge, d. at sea, Pacific.
	Malcolm (Rory)	Eldon.
	Willliam	Eldon. Lost at sea, P.E.I. to Liverpool.
Campbell	Neil	Uigg, killed by train, Oakland, California, when about to board his ship.
	Alex. A.	Pinette, d. New Zealand.
	Roderick A.	Pinette, frozen, crossing Pictou to P.E.I.

	Allan A.	Pinette. Lost in English ship *Androina*, New York to Calcutta.
	Hector A.	Pinette. Lost with all hands in English ship, Bombay to Liverpool.
	Norman	Pinette.
MacRae	Thomas	d. on ship *Northumberland*.
	David	d. in New York.
	Roderick	Pinette, d. Pinette.
	Daniel	Pinette, supt. Edison Co., Chicago.
MacDougall	Duncan	d. Eldon.
	Angus	d. Charlottetown.
	Charles	Pinette, d. Newtown Bridge.
Nicholson	John C.	Orwell Cove, d. Charlottetown.
	John A.	Orwell Cove, d. Orwell Cove.
Macpherson	John	Pinette, d. Medicine Hat.
	Malcolm	Pinette, d. Western Canada.
Macdonald	Malcolm	Uigg, merchant, Georgetown.
MacEachern	Archibald	Eldon, drowned, Brisbane.
Finlayson	Allan	d. Charlottetown.
Young	Thomas	d. Pinette.
	Angus	Drowned off Belle River, P.E.I.
Mackenzie	Roderick	Merchant, Pinette.
Morrison	Hector	Pinette, d. California.

MacLean	Malcolm	Surrey, lost with all hands barquetine *Vigilant*, Baltimore to London.
	Lachlan	Wood Islands; in U.S.
Brown	Angus	d. Wood Islands.
Macinnis	Daniel	Pinette, d. smallpox on brig *Glencairn* in S. Atlantic.
Gillis	John	Orwell Cove.
Shaw	Alex	Lorne Valley. Murdered at sea on barque *Veronica*, mobile to Buenos Aires, by mutinous sailors who were convicted of murder and hanged in Liverpool.

Coasting Captains Out of Belfast

Finlayson	Murdoch	Retired.
	Archibald	d. Point Prim.
Macdonald	Don Hector	d. Pinette.
	John J.	d. Orwell.
McInnis	Alex.	d. Pinette.
MacLean	John	d. Point Prim.
MacRae	Donald D.	Master mariner, d. Pinette.
	Donald	Pinette, son of Donald D., Master of barque *J.H. Myrick* about 1880.
MacDougall	J.	Belle River.
Murchison	Don Neil	d. Point Prim
Nicholson	Roderick	d. Orwell

	Samuel	Mount Buchanan, master of large passenger ship *Glenelg* about 1880. London to Aust.
	Malcolm	Brother of Samuel, master of large passenger ship about 1880.
MacMillan	_____	Master of brig *Alpheta* about 1880.
Riley	John	Belle River.

It took a century of incessant toil to convert the wilderness into the garden we know today. Looking back to the end of their first century in Belfast there is discernible in the social life of the people a condition that may have been developing for some time and which, in any event, became marked with the passing of the years. The large family that had hitherto been a characteristic of the district was no longer seen.

In the early pioneer days there was such variety of farm work that young children were able to earn their living. Their labor was an important factor in clearing the land, in building better homes and thereby in promoting higher standards of living. As there was no time for folly, children were no problem. Society was not disturbed then as it is today by the tyranny of youth. Economic conditions thus encouraged the large family. But when the forests were cleared and the self binder and other modern farm machines were introduced, the situation underwent a change. The demand for manual labor diminished and soon it was apparent that the family was becoming smaller. The elder son usually inherited the homestead and the others migrated to the cities where they found work and were paid according to their individual skills. Another factor that had some bearing on the decline in population was the growing disinclination to marry. Whatever the cause, the effects are startling, for a district that once poured forth a steady stream of young men and women of Celtic origin is now receiving additions from other peoples. The first great surge has spent itself and the depopulation of the district is so marked as to excite in those who love the Gael the gloomy reflection that this once thriving Highland settlement has passed its zenith and is heading for, if not approaching, dissolution.

But many Highland characteristics still remain to remind the visitor of an age long past. A tour of Belfast today is like a visit to the Highlands generations ago. It could not well be otherwise, for during the existence of the settlement the inhabitants have lived in isolation. They have intermarried until almost every family is related. All not native to the island were "foreigners." Old Highland customs, traditions and superstitions were handed down from generation to generation. Family and personal idiosyncracies were marked.

Even the climate favored the continuance of their historic mode of life and thought. Nature was cruel, the ocean stormy, the forests gloomy, the climate harsh. Everything bore omens of disaster. There was little of the gaiety that attends life in more genial climes. It was in fact much like the land they had forsaken.

But though the life of the individual is transitory, that of a people is eternal; and notwithstanding the fact that the population of Belfast is less than it was a century ago, there still remain thousands of descendants of these pioneers scattered to the four corners of the earth. These maintain what is best of the Gaelic culture and play a worthy part in the life of the various communities in which they live.

Dr. Angus Macaulay

There is probably no list extant of those who arrived in Belfast in 1803, but a memorial, dated November 5, 1811, presented to the governor of the colony contains the names of most of the pioneers then living, as well as some who reached manhood after arriving, and others who arrived after 1803.

Among those chosen by Selkirk to assist in his scheme of emigration was Dr. Angus Macaulay of Skye. They were corresponding in 1802 and perhaps earlier. Possessed of an excellent education, force of character and some training in business, the Doctor was well qualified to play an important role in the undertaking. He had been factor for Lord Macdonald, in Skye for several years, and lived at Aird House, Kilmaluag in Trotternish. In this situation he became known to a large portion of the population and was thus in a position to influence those desiring to emigrate, in their choice of destination.

The Macaulays trace their descent from Donald Cam (Blind Donald) Macaulay, tacksman of Brenish, Uig, Lewis, who flourished about 1610. His son Angus was a notable man in his day. He had among others, two sons, Dugald and Donald. Dugald was father of Rev. Aulay Macaulay, minister of Harris, from whom was descended the famous Lord Macaulay. Donald had a son, Rev. Donald, first Presbyterian minister of the Parish of Kilmuir in Skye, in 1700 and later of Bracadale, Skye, until his death, March 3, 1748. He was born about 1674 and graduated, M.A. from Edinburgh University in 1692. His wife was Catherine Macqueen. Among their children was Rev. Aeneas Macaulay, born 1704, who graduated M.A. from Edinburgh University. In 1731 he was ordained minister to Applecross, where he died in 1760. He was regarded as one of the ablest clergymen of his day. His wife was Mary Macleod of Skye. They had twelve children of whom the youngest was Angus (Æneas), later of Belfast, P.E. Island, who was born in 1759 shortly before his father's death.

He graduated M.A. from Glasgow University, attended Divinity Hall, Marischal College, Aberdeen University, 1783-5.

> These certify that Mr. Angus Macaulay, Student of Divinity has attended the Divinity Hall of Marischal College for seventeen meetings of the present session, that he delivered a discourse with approbation and that as far as I know, he has all along behaved himself in a manner every way suitable to the character of a Student of Divinity.
>
> Given at Marischal College the 12th day of March, 1783 by
>
> > Geo. Campbell S.S.T.P.

The minutes of meeting of Presbytery of Skye, Church of Scotland, held at Sconser on December 3, 1783, refer to Mr. Macaulay. They record the following ministers in attendance:

Mr. Donald Mackinnon, Moderator.

Messrs. Donald Macqueen
William Macqueen
Malcolm MacCaskill
John Nicholson
Martin Macpherson
absent Roderick Macleod
William Bethune

Mr. Donald Macqueen was chosen Moderator, and Mr. Malcolm MacCaskill, Clerk p.t.

Æneas Macaulay, who was student of Divinity at the time, delivered a lecture on John 14: 1-3 which was approved. Then the Presbytery prescribed further work for him which he gave in at the next meeting at the same place on 6 April, 1785. The Presbytery being satisfied with his trials licensed him to preach the Gospel.

About this time Mr. Macaulay was teaching school in Skye. India was then attracting many able young men, and Angus Macaulay among them. Wishing to go thither he was corresponding with his cousin Angus Macaulay, living at 67 Charlotte St., Rathbone Place, London, brother of Zachary Macaulay (father of Lord Macaulay) then an official in India. An elder brother of Rev. Angus, named Aulay, had obtained a commission in 1778, in the 78 Seaforth Highlanders and in 1781 had gone to India with his regiment. There, a few years later, he was killed in a duel. For a short time prior to 1789 Rev. Angus was tacksman of Flodigarry, Skye.

By writing bearing date December 10, 1789, Alexander, Lord Macdonald, did "Constitute and Appoint Mr. Angus McAulay, Schoolmaster, of Portree, to be my Factor" in the barony of Trotternish, Skye. Among papers in possession of Dr. Macaulay's descendants, the Murchisons of Pinette River, Point Prim, are letters that reveal strained relations existed between the proprietor and his factor in 1794. They also show that both men had at least a working knowledge of Latin, for to maintain secrecy they sometimes drifted into that language to foil the inquisitive who, they complained, were opening their letters in transit.

About this time the Doctor was recruiting for the Army as well as seeking a commission for himself. An undated letter from him to one Brownrigg, probably a broker, reveals the strange fact that a clergyman would endeavour to raise troops and that he would seek a reward in money or promotion for so doing. A Chaplaincy was highly valued judging by the price paid by the Doctor.

Sir:

I had the honor of your letter of 2nd ... [illegible] wherein you desire me to apply to Mr. Lawrie for 5 pounds per man raised for Major McDonald's corps. This is so inadequate to my disbursements that it will absolutely ruin me and weak family.

But I know his Royal Highness the Duke of York is just and having once acknowledged that my case deserves consideration, I trust his Royal Highness will give me compensation for my expenses and personal trouble as by letter using his authority in my possession. I am absolutely commanded to give up my recruits when a friend would have given me 25 guineas for each of their parents — would have paid my disbursements for their discharge. I have raised 22 hardy Highlanders which exceeds the greatest number raised for a Chaplaincy. I am willing to raise a few more on the same terms — [illegible] — and other officers do or if I obtained the sale or price of an Ensigney it would in part enable me with the Bounty. I shall relinquish my claim and I trust that my — [illegible] my profession and the distance I came, 600 miles — [illegible] with his Royal humanity I trust you will send me an answer with first convenience.

I have the honor to be, Yours,
A. Macaulay.

Receipt

We have received of you £200 for which you have our receipt, also a letter from Mr. Lawrie promising to pay us £350 on your being gazetted chaplain, these two sums making £550 which is the price agreed upon between us for the Chaplaincy of the 78 [indistinct] Regt. which we engage to procure for you within the time specified in Mr. Lawrie's letter.

We are sir,
Your obed. servants
Northumberland St.,
Castleman & Gore
March 22, 1796
To the Rev. Angus Macaulay

On the 24th March, 1797 he was appointed Chaplain to Major General John Whyte's Regiment.

Although about forty years of age Mr. Macaulay decided to study medicine and so attended classes at Glasgow University where he graduated M.D. in 1803. A few months later he was in Belfast, P.E. Island.

Once settled in his new home he threw himself with all his energy into the development of his adopted land. As minister and physician he found much to do. But his vision extended far beyond the horizons of the little colony in which he lived. The tide of immigration was swelling. People were flocking into the new world from all lands. The demand was for land free from the exactions of the landlord. There is something pathetic about the haunting fear in which the settler held the landlord. They had been harassed by landlordism in the homeland and were resentful of the servitude it entailed. They wanted none of it in the new world. Nothing less than freehold land would satisfy them. Being a man of foresight Dr. Macaulay soon sensed the feelings of the people and the significance of the flood of immigration then pouring into America. He made an arduous journey through Nova Scotia and Cape Breton Island seeking suitable free land on which to establish a colony. As a result of this journey he submitted the following petition:

> To His Honor Brigadier General Nepean President of His Majesty's Council and Commander in Chief in and over Cape Breton and its Dependencies etc etc etc
>
> The Petition of Angus Macaulay M.D. Most respectfully Sheweth
>
> That Your Honor's Petitioner came four years ago to Prince Edward Island at the Head of upwards of four hundred

Protestants from Scotland whom many have followed since, now forming a respectable Colony

That the land of said Island being now all private property leaves no encouragement for the rapid increase of population in said Colony as its exertions are damped by the land Proprietors or their Stewarts

That the Petitioner has been desired by several in said Island also had numerous applications from Europe to procure a place of settlement for men who will undoubtedly be lost to the British Empire unless an Assylum be opened for them upon Kings land; he has applications also from an influx of Emigrants floating about Pictou, etc.

That Your Honor's Petitioner at a considerable expense travelled a part of Nova Scotia and came also here from Prince Edward Island to look out for an eligible Situation

That he thinks the natural advantages of Soil & Fisheries of this Province a sufficient inducement for colonization especially around the Lake Bradore and its tributary streams

That those whom he wishes first to introduce are industrious protestants, loyal subjects

That to promote the object he has in view it is requisite to have Kings land in proportion to the Progress of the Colony according to the rules which are or may hereafter appear proper to Your Honor in Council.

That to facilitate the Progress of the Colony and to prevent circuitous and dangerous navigation to Emigrants from Prince Edward Island etc — and also to induce them gradually and successively to pour into the Bradore and its Rivers it is humbly suggested and Requested of Your Honor that a Tract of Land on each side of the Madavecuk or Indian River be reserved for the Colony for a twelve month and during that period to be given in Lots to those to be brought forward by the Petitioner.

That also The Petitioner obtain for himself one thousand acres in an eligible situation upon said River in order to facilitate and open a regular communication through the N.W. Peninsula of this province from the Settlement at Margarie into the Bradore as his object is to Colonize rapidly not only upon the Course of said River but also upon the Lake. So confident is he of success that he shall be the first to begin next summer or earlier and shall relinquish his Prospects as Physician & Clergyman in Prince Edward

Island for the Promotion of this Colony — So far does his private inclinations and the Public benefit embrace one the other and if he is at first fortunate enough to be countenanced by Your Honor the Petitioner has no doubt of the final result —

That tho' the Petitioner's first Steps will be slow from his private concerns for a few months yet they will gradually be accelerated to a surprising degree as the means, and the end he has in view will gradually stimulate and prop each other if he is encouraged to direct and to divert the current of industrious and Loyal Emigrants to the natural advantages which this Province holds forth to unfettered exertions not paralized by indolent and monopolizing Land Proprietors of the uncultivated Wilderness in North America

Your Honors Petitioner as in Duty bound
will ever Pray
Sydney 30th July, 1807
Angus Macaulay,
Chaplain upon the retired pay of the 1st. W.I. Regmt.

[Endorsed on the Back]

Petition of Doctor Macaulay
Complied with 3rd August 1807
W. McKinnon Clerk Council

Nothing ever came of this proposed plan for the Doctor continued to live in Belfast actively engaged in public and private affairs. But the worthy physician was restless and a few years later we find him representing his case to the Governor of the Colony in the following terms:

> To His Excellency Joseph Frederic Wallet Des Barres Colonel in His Majesty's Army Lieutenant Governor and Commander in Chief in and over His Majesty's Island Prince Edward and the territories thereunto adjacent Chancellor and Vice Admiral of the same &c— &c— &c—
>
> The Memorial and representation of the Reverend Angus Macaulay.
>
> Most respectfully showeth
>
> That your memorialist was appointed Chaplain to Major General John Whyt's Regiment as will more fully appear by his commission lodged in your Excellency's Private Secretary's Office bearing date the 24th of March, 1797.
>
> Your memorialist perceiving by the official

communication through your Excellency from the Right Honorable Secretary at War enclosing the "Terms of Service of Army Chaplains" dated "War Office 21st December 1809" signifying "that every Army Chaplain is to have a commission rendering him liable to serve when called upon either on a military station in Great Britain or elsewhere, or with any part of the army on Foreign service for the term of eight years."

Your memorialist therefore begs leave to represent through your Excellency that he has been placed for a series of years on half pay at the rate of four shillings per diem notwithstanding it has always been the wish and desire of your memorialist to be employed on Actual Duty, and in consequence thereof has held and still holds himself in readiness when called on to proceed to such Service.

Your memorialist has not for any period since being placed on half pay, although totally inadequate to the support of his numerous family, engaged in any care or occupation, nor has he accepted any living, or other preferment or entered into any engagement incompatible with his military situation.

On the arrival of your Memorialist on

this Island he found himself surrounded by a numerous population from the Highlands of Scotland, under indigent circumstances, who understood no other than the Gaelic Language. Your Memorialist therefore as in Duty bound to support the Christian Establishment and that of regular Society has ever since officiated as a clergyman without any manner of perquisite emolument or remuneration whatsoever.

Your memorialist hath not only confined himself to the faithful discharge of the duty he conceived incumbent on him in the Parish of Saint John's, wherein he resides, but frequently has to travel through other settlements in this government to perform pastoral offices; a task imposed on your memorialist in consequence of there being no other clergyman of the reformed church on this Island who understands the Gaelic language. The services of your memorialist will more fully appear to your Excellency by the annexed document under the signature of the principal of the inhabitants of Saint John's Parish.

Your memorialist furthermore begs leave to mention that as he has always made his profession his study he is induced to anticipate the hope of a favorable result to this

his application through the interest of your Excellency's influence by laying his case before the Right Honorable the Secretary at War—soliciting that he may be attached to the Army agreeable to the Terms stated in the official communication or considered as deserving some relief from His Majesty's Bounty as to His Royal Wisdom may seem meet; and your memorialist as in Duty bound will ever pray &c—&c—&c—

Angus Macaulay Chaplain
By His Excellency Joseph Frederick Wallet Des Barres Colonel etc.
J. F. Des Barres

Great Seal

I certify that the appointment and services of the Reverend Angus Macaulay are justly stated in the aforegoing memorial and accompanying document and that in the performance of his religious duties as a clergyman in this Government his conduct has been exemplary, diligent, and zealous, and having a numerous family I most humbly beg leave to recommend him for generous consideration.

Given under my hand and Seal at Arms at

Charlottetown this first day of March in the year of our Lord 1813, and in the 53rd year of His Majesty's Reign. By His Excellency's Command

J. L. Des Barres Pr. Secretary

COPY OF APPOINTMENT OF MR. MACAULAY

I, Alexander Lord MacDonald, heritable proprietor of the lands Barony after mentioned—Do hereby CONSTITUTE and APPOINT Mr. Angus Macaulay, Schoolmaster of Portree to be my Factor to the effect after specified giving and hereby granting to him my full power warrant and Commission for me and in my name and behalf to uplift levy and receive all and sundry the tack-duties, feu-duties, tythe-duties and other rents, maills, farms, kaims, customs, casualties and other customs profits and duties payable and presentable to me by the Vasals, Tacksmen, Tenants and possessors. My said lands and barony of Trotternish lying in the parishes of Kilmuir, Snizort and Portree, Island of Sky and Sheriffdom of Inverness, and for the current crop and year 1789 and preceeding arrears if any be as well as in time coming during the continuance hereof, And with full power to the said Angus McAulay to call and sue for payment of the said Tack-duties and other rents profits and duties of the said lands and Barony of Trotternish obtain Decreets therefore either in his own name or mine cause put the same in execution and upon payment in whole or in part to grant discharges and receipts thereof which shall be as binding and obligatory as if granted by myself and generally every other thing in relation to the premises to do which I could do myself if present.

PROVIDING always as it is hereby expressly provided and declared that the said Angus MacAulay shall be obliged so oft as he shall be required to hold compt to me for his whole intremissions in virtue hereof after deduction of the charges of such legal diligence as may be needful for recovery of the said rents and other necessary expenses of management and reasonable gratification for his pains and trouble and for more security I consent to the registering thereof in the books of Council and Sassine or any other Judge books comptent thereon to remain for My procurators for the purpose

In witness whereof I subscribe this and the

preceding pages written on stamped paper by Peter Halkesston, Clerk, to William MacEwan, writer in Edinburgh, at Edinburgh the tenth day of December, 1789, before these witnesses the said William MacEwan and Allan McGilleveray my servant.

      (Sgd.) McDonald
   (Sgd.) William MacEwan, Witness
  (Sgd.) Allan McGilleveray, Witness

In addition to his many other activities, Dr. MacAulay became a member of the legislative assembly of Prince Edward Island, of which body he was Speaker for several years. His portrait hangs in the legislative chamber in Charlottetown. He had the liberal and tolerant outlook that characterized his forbears. His father was brought before the general assembly of his church on a charge of heresy of which he was acquitted. Consistent with these liberal principles he actively espoused Catholic emancipation at a time when such a stand was unpopular. Other liberal measures, many of them in advance of the spirit of the age, received the energetic support of the Doctor.

Dr. Macaulay married Mary MacDonald at Borniscutag, Skye, in February, 1790. She was daughter of Capt. Samuel MacDonald of Sartil, Skye, son of Somerled of Sartil, son of Sir James

Mor Macdonald, 2nd Baronet of Sleat, chief of the clan. He had gone to North Carolina with his family and relatives, in or about 1771, joined the Royal Highland Emigrant Regiment, the 184th, as Capt., and in 1776 was taken prisoner in the Battle of Moore's Creek, N.C. He was exchanged and rejoined his regiment in Nova Scotia, where he was at Shelburne in 1787. He returned to Skye and on his death was on the half-pay list of retired officers with the rank of lieutenant. When about 93, he married his second wife, Catherine Stewart, then a young girl of about 22. For a man of this great age he had the unusual record of leaving three sons by this marriage.

The London *Times* of November 7, 1830, records Capt. Samuel's death as follows: "Died at his house, in the Parish of Kilmuir, Isle of Skye, on the 10th ult. Lieutenant Soirle Macdonald at the very advanced age of 106. He expired not of any particular complaint but merely from decay and exhaustion. He left three children under ten years of age."

Dr. Macaulay and his wife, Mary, had a family of six children who reached maturity:
1. Charlotte, wife of Angus MacLean, Point Prim, with issue, three children.
2. Flora, unmarried.
3. John, unmarried.
4. William, in Wisconsin, married Miss

Henderson of Ontario, with issue, one child.
5. Ebenezer, died, aged 22, unmarried.
6. Alice, wife of Samuel Murchison, Pinette River, with issue, four children.

Selkirk gave Dr. Macaulay a farm of eleven hundred acres in Point Prim and from it the Doctor donated a few acres for a burial ground. Here this distinguished couple were laid to rest. The headstone records that Angus Macaulay, M.D. died Dec. 6, 1827, and his wife Mary, on April 9, 1857, aged 99.

Names of Settlers

There is no known list of those who settled in Belfast in 1803. But as there were only a few deaths prior to 1811 most of those who signed the following petition were without doubt original settlers. Some were sons who reached maturity subsequent to 1803 and a few were settlers who arrived between 1803 and 1811. This list is among the Macaulay papers in possession of his descendants the Murchisons of Pinette River.

Prince Edward Island November 5, 1811

We the undersigned, beg leave to express our gratitude and respect to the Reverend Doctor Angus Macaulay for his unremitted attention in keeping alive true Christian devotion and piety for seven years among us. The greatest part being unacquainted with the English tongue would be totally deprived of clerical instruction were it not for his knowledge of the Gaelic language. We also bear testimony that he hath at his own expense erected a chapel near his house in St. John's Parish where he officiates weekly (when at home) in the neighborhood of several hundreds Protestant souls, solely indebted, under divine Providence, to him, for the blessings of Public Worship and Christian Baptism. We also testify that he preaches occasionally and Baptises the children of several other settlements in this Island, where the people are in our penurious condition, without the means of making any worldly compensation for his voluntary and pious exertions.

Murdoch Gillis, Elder
Donald Gillis, his X mark
Donald MacRae, his X mark

Evender MacRae, Elder	Angus McDonald
Charles Stewart	Donald Mackinnon
Hector MacDonald X	Allan Shaw
Donald McInnes	Donald Murchison, Elder
Murdoch Maclean X	John McLeod

Donald MacLeod
Donald McPhee
John Murchison
John Macrae
Donald Murchison
Roderick Macrae
Alexn. McLeod
Donald Macrae
John McDonald, Sr. Elder
Kennat McKinzie
John McDonald, Junior
Alexd. McKenzie
John Gillies
Hector Morison
Donald Nicholson, Elder
Donald Macrae
Murdo McLeod
Donald Stewart
Donald McPherson
Alex Martin
Harry McLeod
Charles Stewart
Samuel Martin
John Macpherson
John Nicolson
John Bell
Donald Nicolson
Lachlin MacLean
John McKinsie
Malcolm Bell
John Campbell
Malcolm McMillan
John Ross
James Courie
Donald Beaton X
Donald McNill
Donald Ross

Malcolm Mun
John Beaton
Jas. Currie
Angus Beaton
James Munn
Angus Ness
Odochardy (Angus)
Saml. Beaton
Donald Odochardy
John Gilles
Hector McQuarry
Angus McMillan
John MacLeod
Hector McMillan
John Buchanan
James McMillan
Angus Munn
Allan McMillan
Murdoch Buchanan
Archibald Blue
John Macqueen
Malcom McNeill
Alexander Lamond
Dugald Bell X
Martin Martin
John Mun X
Soirle Nicolson
Angus Barr
Malcom Buchanan
John MacPherson
Donald Buchanan
Finlay MacRae
Donald Macleod
Peter Campbell
Donald Macqueen
Angus Beaton Senr.
Peter Murchison

Kenneth MacKenzie Senr.
Donald MacLeod
John MacRae
Murdoch McDonald
Finlay McRae
Finlay Odochardy
Alexander McArthur
Donald McLeod

Alexander Mc... [illegible]
John McDonald
John MacDonald
Malcolm MacLeod
Alex MacLeod
Donald Martin

Our curiosity is excited to find the Irish name Odochardy in the above list. In his monumental work *The Surnames of Scotland,* Dr. George Fraser Black, head of the Scottish section of the New York Public Library wrote:

> O'Docharty, Irish O'Dochartaigh 'descendant of Dochartach.' There were a number of people of this name in Islay in early seventeenth century under the Campbells of Cawdor. Donald O'Dochartie in Islay, 1629 (Cawdor) James Odocherty and William Odocherty in Tormistall, Islay. 1733 (Bk. Islay p. 552).

Irish records refer to "Sir Cahin O'Dogherty's Rising." They seem to have lived in Ulster, near Derry.

Family tradition has it that the grandfather of the three brothers, Angus, Findlay and Donald Odochardy migrated to Skye, presumably from Islay. The family on P.E. Island changed the name to Dockerty. Angus O'Dockerty married

Catherine McLeod of Glasphein, Pinette River, Belfast. Their son, Malcolm Dockerty, later of Cardigan, married his cousin, Christy Macqueen, of Orwell. Their son, Robert Dockerty, married Adelaid Birt of Mount Stewart. They had three sons: Malcolm Birt Dockerty (b. 1909, M.D., C.M. Dal. U. 1934, gold medalist; M.S. Minnesota U. 1937) Prof. U. of Minn., chief pathologist, St. Mary's Hospital, Mayo Clinic, Rochester, Minn., married Marjorie Stoddart of Jamestown, North Dakota; with John Malcolm, Jr.

John Stewart Mills Dockerty (b. 1911, M.Sc., Dal. U. 1933, with great distinction; Ph.D., U. of Toronto, 1935; National Research Council Fellowship). In research dept., Corning Glass Co., N. Y., married Dorothy Anne Browning, of Edinburgh, with issue.

Cyrus Dockerty (b. 1914) lives on the ancestral farm on St. Peters Road, Cardigan, m. Miss MacSwain, with issue.

It would appear from references in some of Selkirk's letters to Dr. Macaulay that there were "indented men" among the settlers. These would be boys eager to emigrate, but unable to pay the cost of passage. For such Selkirk would advance the necessary money. The relationship of master and servant would exist until the debt was paid. A contract setting out the terms of the agreement would be signed by both parties before the emigrant embarked. This was called indenture, hence the term "indented" men. Thousands of emigrants entered the American colonies under this system to become high class citizens and progenitors of distinguished families.

In a letter from Selkirk to Dr. Macaulay dated Charlottetown, Aug. 11, referring to several matters including a boat which he hired to take the smith, his tools, some coals and boards for the first building in Belfast, he says: "If the boat which these things are sent by, is of material use it may be kept—it is paid for at a dollar a day—if not it should be sent back & if any of the men who navigate it are anxious to remain & look about the country, perhaps some of the indented men may be put in their place to bring her back,—."

And in a letter of Friday, 19th August: "—I found a very intelligent settler[1] up Vernon River who promised to come down and give assistance to our people if he was assisted by their work to make up for the time he should lose. I have therefore desired Mr. Cameron to take two of the indented men, & go up tomorrow to work for him—."

And in a letter of Wednesday: "—J. McKenzie, the overseer goes down by the boat, & will take charge of the indented men—."

1   James Laird, who later married widow Enman, his neighbor.

Origin of the Name Belfast

There has been some uncertainty as to the origin of the place name Belfast. Some have attributed it to a corruption of the Selkirk settlers of an early French place name but such is not the case. In his diary Selkirk made the following entry. "Saturday Augt. 13th. Having finished all the business with the *Dykes* & left her ready for sea & sealed up my letters to go by the post, I set off for the settlement at the old French village called Belfast. I went on board the *Polly*—." It would thus appear that the district was known as Belfast before the settlers arrived in 1803. The true origin of the name appears in a letter from a settler addressed to the editor of the *Gentleman's Magazine* (London, Eng.) dated November 8th, 1770, and published in the issue of that magazine of March, 1771. This letter seems to remove any doubt. Unfortunately the name of the writer, who was a keen observer, was withheld, but as it is of more than passing interest the letter is reproduced as published.

Description of the Island of St. John, in the Gulph of St. Laurence, in a letter from that place, dated November 8th, 1770.

We arrived here safe the middle of August. I have since been over several parts of the

Island, which exceeds in most respects, my expectations. I saw the remains of many barns, and other buildings for farmers, as large as any I remember in Berkshire, and the lands appear to be excellent for wheat, and all sorts of grain and herbage. There are many orchards, which produce very good apples, and other fruits; gooseberries, currants and strawberries seem to be native on the Isle, as they are met with everywhere in abundance. Governor Paterson, and his family arrived a few days after us; I have seen him several times; he seems good-natured, and fit to struggle with the difficulties that must attend the settlement of such an infant colony.

A Man-of-War, called the *Mermaid*, touched here; the Captain has got a fine lot[1] of 20,000 acres, which has the good remains of a village upon it, with a Church; it was called Prim by the French, but he intends to name it Belfast, after a village in Ireland. I mention this circumstance, as I landed on

---

1 The island was divided into lots or townships: Lot 57 was granted by the crown in 1767 to Samuel Smith and Capt. James Smith, R.N. of the *Seahorse*, later of the *Mermaid*. The *Mermaid* commanded by Capt. James Smith anchored at "Port Le-Joya Island of St. John " from the 5th to the 25th August and from the 6th to the 26th October, 1710. (Extract from ship's Log)

the spot, and eat some excellent fruits of his orchard, which though overgrown with weeds produce plenty, and there appear to be six or seven hundred acres of clear land belonging to it; the soil is very deep in many places on the Islands and must produce hemp and flax, but all looks forlorn, for want of cultivation; however, the Island must soon wear a new face, if the proprietors do their duty. There are about three hundred settlers come from England and Scotland this summer. Those from Scotland brought a Presbyterian Parson with them. A very good sort of man. People that come hither from Europe, should set out in April, to have the summer before them, to provide houses and stock for the winter, which is now beginning to set in.

The Island is upwards of 100 miles long, and about 30 or 40 broad, with many fine rivers which intersect the whole, and must make carriage easy. Here I am told there are no fogs, as on the continent, which is a good circumstance.

I wish other people were animated with the same spirit for settlement that I am; if that was the case, I think this Island, in a very few years, would make a great figure in the exports of corn, fish, pork, etc., but am afraid it will be kept back by people at home, who have got grants without intention of settling the land. I am in treaty for half a lot, or 10,000 acres, and expect to get it cheaper than if I had purchased in London. I now act with my eyes open, knowing the situation and quality of the land, to be good. We can have cattle, pigs, sheep and other stock from the Continent, on very easy terms; those who bring out coarse woolens and other goods fit for this climate, and an infant colony must make great profit on them—I would not have people come without some small property or a knowledge of husbandry, fishery, building, smith's work etc.—idle folks will not do here. Fish is amazing plenty around the Island; the Cod fishery must be very valuable in time, but my scheme you know is farming.

To the above by way of footnote may be added the following: The ship *Falmouth*, John McWhae, Master; Buchanan, Morrison and Company, of Greenock, owners, sailed from Greenock, at 5 P.M. on April 8, A. D. 1770, and came to anchor in Richmond Bay, St. Johns Island (later P.E.I.) about 2 P.M. on June 2nd.

The *Falmouth* carried a party of Scottish emigrants. Among their names appear Brown, Auld,

Jamieson, Lawson, McGregor, McLaughlan, McCallum and other well known pioneer families. These settlers were accompanied by a Presbyterian minister, the Rev. William Drummond who labored on the Island for at least a year, perhaps longer. He kept a diary and from a copy of same, now in the hands of Ira M. Brown of Charlottetown, P.E.I. a descendant of [Unknown Given Name] Brown, one of the passengers, these facts are gleaned. It is possible that the *Falmouth* was the first ship to arrive on the Island with an organized party of emigrants from Britain and that Mr. Drummond was the first Presbyterian minister to labor for his church in that colony.

Robert Jones

Robert Jones, son of Willlam Jones and his wife, Margaret Locke, was born at Hawkhead Mills, near Paisley, Scotland, in 1776. His wife was Hannah Simpson, of West Kilbride, Scotland. They moved to London, England, shortly after their marriage. In 1809 he migrated to Prince Edward Island. Mr. Jones was a trained draughtsman and cabinet maker having spent seven years in that calling. On arriving in Charlottetown he engaged with Waters & Birnie[1], general and shipping mer-

---

1   George Birnie was agent for the Alliance British and Foreign Life Insurance Office, London, England.

chants. In 1811 he was joined by his wife and four children. His diary records that in 1812 he spent 58 days surveying lumber on the ship *Princess of Wales*, and worked on board as shipjoiner for 44 days. In 1813 he was made surveyor of lumber on P.E. Island. In 1815, and perhaps earlier, he was operating Lord Selkirk's mill on Pinette River. In 1816 he disposed of the lease and returned to Charlottetown. Shortly thereafter he took up land in Lot 49, where he resided until his death in 1859 and where some of his descendants have resided continuously ever since. He is buried in Alexandra churchyard, near Pownal.

In the meantime, in 1820 he was appointed captain of a company in the 7th battalion of militia and in 1825 was appointed commissioner of highways for Lots 48, 49, 50 and 55.

Mr. Jones was much trusted by his employers and friends. Many sought his advice. He made sketches and plans for a courthouse in Charlottetown and erected other buildings there. He was a skilled craftsman, took pride in his work and earned a name for honesty, integrity and industry. In all respects he exemplified what is best in Scottish character and tradition. Methodical and exact in all his ways he kept a diary in fine handwriting recording the daily activities in which he engaged. These entries give an interesting sidelight on life in the various communities in which he lived and worked.

Reference to Mr. Jones appears elsewhere on these pages under the heading of church and mills.

It is worthy of mention that J. Walter Jones (b. 1878; M.A. Acadia U.) son of James Benjamin Jones and his wife Maria Isabel Stewart, was premier of P.E.I. for several years. In June 1953 he was called to the Senate. He died of a heart attack in his office in the Senate building on March 31, 1954.

In the *Guardian*, of October 26, 1949, appeared the following extract from the *Islander*, a discontinued local newspaper.

Point Prim Lighthouse

On Monday last, a Committee appointed by the House of Assembly, consisting of the Hon. Joseph Pope, Speaker, F. Longworth, W. Douse, G. Coles, A. MacLean and D. Montgomery, Esqs., accompanied by the Hon. T. H. Haviland, W. Cundall, Esq., High Sheriff, L.W. Gall, Esq., Land Surveyor, and J. D. Macdonnell, W. Bremner, George Birnie, J. Longworth, F. Kempster, J. Davis, Jr., R. Finlayson, T. Pethick, J. Davis, Sr., K. Dogherty and Isaac Smith, Esqs., and the two Masters Douse, proceeded, in ten sleighs, to Point Prim, for the purpose of selecting a site for the intended Light House.

The party left the Queen's Wharf about ten, and after crossing the Portage to Belle Vue, drove out on the ice in a direct line about thirteen miles to Point Prim. On landing, a site was chosen for the building, which commands a beautiful view of some thirty miles on the Straits of Northumberland, the different points at that distance being easily distinguished ... The land was surveyed by Mr. Gall, and the clearing of the woods for the building disposed of to persons from the neighboring settlements.

The party partook of a lunch and returned the sixteen miles, in one hour and twenty minutes, thus showing the facility with which travelling can be performed on good ice in winter.

We may observe that the site for the building was given by the Right Hon. the Earl of Selkirk through his Land Agent, Wm. Douse, Esq., and will add much to the improvement, as well as to the importance of that part of his Lordship's property. The House of Assembly have provided a grant of money for its erection, and the work will be commenced forthwith.

—*The Islander*
April 5, 1845.

This lighthouse is still in use in 1957.

In the columns of the same newspaper, a few months earlier, J.L.M., a correspondent, recalled some early events recorded by Dougald Henry, who was born in Malpeque, in 1817. While working as a smith for Thomas Robertson, of Charlottetown, about 1846, the latter had the contract to build the above lighthouse. Henry was one of those sent to the Point to put up the lantern. On Governor's Island there was a spar light on which they used to hoist a lantern by hand.

Settlers in Lots 49 and 50

Apart from MacMillan, Fraser and MacLeod there was no one living on the south side of Orwell Bay when the Selkirk settlers arrived in 1803. Their nearest neighbors were the Loyalists who had arrived from the American colonies some years earlier and made homes in Lots 49 and 50 on the north side of the Bay. These were unusually industrious, intelligent and successful pioneers. From them, for the first few critical years, the Scots got essential supplies of food and foundation stock of sheep, swine, poultry, horses and cattle.

Campbell's *History of P.E. Island* lists the inhabitants of Lots 49 and 50 in 1798 as follows:

Lot 49

	Total Members in Family
John McGinnis	8
William Hassard	8
William Jetson	9
Barney McCrossen	4
John Burho	11
William Wood, Jr.	2
William Wood, Snr.	10
Joseph Smith	7
John Costin	6
John Eacharn	7
Nics. Jenkins	11
Geo. Hayden	3
James L. Hayden	8

Lot 50

… Reynolds	2
Joseph Beers, Esq.	6
Frederick Praught	7
Richard Myers	8
Tho. Pendergast	7
James Carver	7
Peter Musick	7
Spencer Crane	4
Don. McPhee	7
John Praught	2
John McDonald	4

William Young	11
James Lard	7
William Laws	2
John Van Niderstine	5
John Haley	1
Geo. Coughlin	4
Win. Morris	4
John Monlin	1
Fred Schultze	2

Joseph Beers, Esq.

In a report to Governor Sir Guy Carlton, Col. Morse lists among those about to settle on St. John's Island, in June, 1784, several officers of the disbanded First Battalion of the King's Rangers. Of these John Throckmorton, a captain and Joseph Beer (or Beers), an ensign settled near each other in Cherry Valley. The dwelling in which Beers entertained Selkirk overnight, a pretentious structure in its day, still stands, a token of good taste and confidence in the future.

Capt. Beer's second wife was Margaret Hayden, who was born in New York State in 1776. They had six children.

James L. Hayden

Cherry Valley was named by James Lewis Hayden after Cherry Valley (near Mohawk Valley) in New York State, where he had lived and where a creek perpetuates the family name today. He was born on May 25, 1749, of German parents. In November, 1778, during the Revolutionary War their settlement was raided by Butler's Rangers, a British detachment under the Tory, John Butler, and Indian allies under the famous chief, Joseph Brant. These raiders massacred about fifty persons. Being loyal to Britain, Hayden was so harassed by the revolting colonists that in despair he abandoned his home and with his wife, whose maiden name was Haas or Hoss, and three helpless children, set out for New York where they arrived May 29, 1780.

Charles MacMillan and his sister, Maria, both of Vernon River descendants of James Lewis Hayden, possess the German family Bible and the journal kept by the methodical Mr. Hayden, in which is recorded the unhappy wanderings that finally brought the family to P.E. Island. The following extracts are from this journal:

> April 16, 1774, George Hadin, born and baptized by Mr. Sayre (?) His sureties his mother – parents. May 29, 1780, com to New York.

Sept., 20, 1783, left New York for Shelborne, N.S., and landed there October 4, 1783, and com to Island of Saint John, June 11th, 1785.

The family Bible records the names of their children:

1. George Hayden, born April 16, 1774.
2. Margaret Hayden, born March 18, 1776.
3. Elizabeth Hayden, born September 28, 1778.
4. Jacob Lewis Hayden, born November 25, 1780, d. N. Y. January 6, 1783.
5. Catherine Hayden, born January 28, 1783.
6. James Hayden, born July 5, 1786. Born Lot 49, P.E.I., moved to V. R. [Vernon River]
7. Alex. Lewis Hayden, born April 2, 1788.
8. Ann Hayden, born July 26, 1790.
9. William Hayden, born December 22, 1792.
10. Maria Hayden, born September 4, 1795.
11. Frederick Hayden, born November 15, 1798, d. July 4, 1810.

On April 7, 1796, Mr. Hayden took a 99-year lease of a hundred acre farm on Mill Creek in Cherry Valley, from the proprietor, the widow of Robert Clark, a London merchant. On April 7, 1801, he assigned this lease to John Acorn, who had a mill on Vernon River which he seems to have abandoned owing to a defective title. Hayden took over the Vernon River mills shortly thereafter. For over a century his descendants operated these mills, both grist and saw, with success. The last member of the family in possession was John Hayden, who died about thirty years ago. James Lewis Hayden finally passed away in 1832. His wife died on May 10, 1837. They were members of the Episcopal church, but latterly the family in Vernon River adhered to the Methodist church.

In his diary Selkirk records that "Hayden, Millwright near Charlotte Town, gave me an estimate for Mills on 58 or 57…"

Miss Elizabeth MacRae, of Waterside, Pownal Bay, a descendant of James L. Hayden, recently wrote of her Hayden relations and some of their neighbors as follows:

> Four Hayden brothers occupied a tract of land extending from near Pownal easterly towards Millview. George, the eldest lived on the farm adjoining on the east the Macrae farm. He was married but left no children.
>
> Margaret Hayden, eldest daughter of J. L. Hayden, was wife of Major Joseph Beer of Cherry Valley. They had six children.
>
> Elizabeth Hayden was wife of Mr. Auld, of Covehead. On his death she married Mr. Miller. Their son, Lemuel Miller, was

Principal of West Kent School, Charlottetown.

Catherine Hayden was wife of Thomas Mellish.

Ann Hayden was wife of Mr. Wisener.

Maria Hayden was wife of Alexander MacMillan, Alberry Plains. Of their family, Charles MacMillan and Maria MacMillan now live in Charlottetown; Rev. Dr. Frederick MacMillan (M.A.), for many years rector of a Reading, Penna. Episcopal Church and his sister Melinda MacMillan, a retired school teacher, live in Philadelphia; Henry Hyde MacMillan, an engineer, lives in Detroit.

James Hayden operated a store and shipyard in Vernon River. His wife was a sister of Robert Furness, a Yorkshireman who settled at Vernon River Bridge. Their son Lemuel Cambridge Hayden, owned and lived on the farm beside the mills. His first wife was Janetta Ross (1841-1882), daughter of Donald Ross, of Uigg and his wife Flora, daughter of Donald Nicholson, Steinshole, miller on Orwell River, with issue, Mary B. Hayden, Belmont, Mass., and Charlotte P. Hayden, Exeter, New Hampshire, both unmarried, and Sidney (d. 1954), Vancouver, in Marine Department, Ottawa, married Miss Nickerson, of Nova Scotia, with issue

Cuthbert. Lemuel C. Hayden, married secondly, Margaret MacLeod, daughter of William MacLeod "Sengie," Vernon River Bridge and his wife, Christiana MacLeod, sister of John McLeod of Glasphein McLeods, with issue, Stella (Mrs. H. D. MacLennan) and Adelaide (Mrs. F. J. Chappell) both of Ch'town, and Helen (Mrs. F. F. McKinley) Sydney, N.S.

James Hayden, brother of Lemuel, married Margaret Ross (1839-1918) sister of above Janetta Ross, with issue, two sons. They lived in California.

WILLIAM JETSON

This refers to the Judson family of Alexandra, near Pownal. The family originated in Newcastle-on-Tyne, England, spent some time in Carolina, whence they came to the Island. Jacob, one of the family, married Mary MacLeod of Kinross. Their son, John, a physician, died at Alexandra a few years ago.

JOHN BURHO

The Burho family of Alexandra is a branch of the Brehaut family that came from the Channel Islands and settled in 1806, in Guernsey Cove, near Murray Harbor, P.E.I. A branch of the family live at Lyndale, near Kinross.

Several other Guernsey families came to P.E. Island at the same time. Until they were able to erect their own homes these excellent settlers occupied premises provided by Mr. Cambridge, an English shipbuilder, at Murray Harbor. Among them one finds the family names, Le Lacheur, Roberts, Nicolle, de Jersey, Marquand, Machon and others.

John Eachern

The first member of the family to arrive on the Island was John Acorn, of Danforth, Maine. His father Mathias was a German from Hesse-Darmstadt. According to family tradition the name was Eichorn in Germany. For generations the family were millers. John fought in the American Revolutionary war in the British army. He emigrated to the Island in or about 1782, still a young man. He is said to have received a grant of land in Vernon River and started a mill about 1786. About 1801 he moved to Cherry Valley where he operated a saw and grist mill that descended in the family to his great-grandson, Seaforth Acorn, and the latter's son, Everett Acorn, and was owned by them until recently. While living in Vernon River John Acorn married Eleanor, daughter of a retired

British officer living in Nova Scotia. They had 13 children. John died in 1857, aged 96. His wife died many years earlier. Both are buried in the Methodist cemetery in Pownal.

James Laird

This refers to James Laird, who had a comfortable home when Selkirk called on him in Vernon River. He is referred to on another page in an extract from Selkirk's diary as a Loyalist from Carolina. Writing Dr. Macaulay on Friday, 19th August, 1803, the Earl refers to him: "... I found a very intelligent settler up Vernon River who promised to come down and give assistance to our people if he was assisted by their work to make up for the time he should lose. I have therefore desired Mr. Cameron to take two of the indented men, and go up tomorrow to work for him. I shall be obliged to you to lend him your canoe, and to let him have two tolerable hands to set out early in the morning up the River ..."

Mr. Laird married Widow Enman, his neighbor, with issue Polly and Margaret. Polly married Angus Ross. A descendant, William Ross, with wife and children live on the Laird homestead in 1957.

John Praught

The family tradition is that this Loyalist family originated in Holland or Germany and that the name there was Praacht. The wife of the original settler in Lot 50 was Susannah Wagner, from Germany.

John Van Niderstine

The Vaniderstines were a Loyalist family of Dutch extraction. They settled near the headwaters of Vernon River and were highly respected.

Peter Musick

Peter Musick settled at what was formerly known as Gallows Point on land now owned by descendants of Joseph Tweedy. According to Campbell's history of P.E.I., he had four sons and three daughters living in 1798. A son, John, married Thankful Gay, sister of the three brothers Henry, John and Ephraim Gay and had issue, among others, Sarah, who married John Cavanagh, son of John Cavanagh, Sr. and his wife Mathilde Beer. Their daughter, Thankful, married and her daughter, Lotta C. R., is wife of Melvin A. Dunham, of Burlington, Mass.

Peter Musick (d. January 15, 1918, aged 82), son

of said John, settled in Kinross, where he married Catherine (d. March 8, 1915, aged 75), daughter of Donald Kelley, native of Stornoway, Lewis, first teacher in Uigg school. They had seven children, of whom a son Henry, (b. July 11, 1863, died Dec 1, 1951), lived on the old homestead. Married with issue. Howard (b. 1865) lived and died in North Dakota, October 31, 1950, married with issue. Another son, William Henry (B.A. McMaster U.), is a retired school inspector in Saskatchewan. His son Gordon, M.D. (U of Man.), born January 15, 1922, practices his profession in Regina, Sask. He is married with issue: Donald, b. Nov. 23, 1948; and Gordon Waynes, b. June 5, 1951. A grandson, Dr. Trevor Waye (McGill U.), is a dentist in Charlottetown.

John Musick married, secondly, Miss Nelson of China Point.

Adelaide Musick, a daughter of Peter Musick I married Stephen Carrier, 1st of the family on P.E.I. Of their children, Peter was the eldest, John and Henry were twins; Stephen II was youngest. He married and had two sons, John and George and eight daughters. John married Christine Bruce of Surrey, Belfast. The twins, John and Henry, Christina recalls, were so alike in appearance that they could not be distinguished apart. They had an unusual affection for each other. So much so that when one of them shot an animal that was destroying their crops and for this offence was committed to gaol, the brother on each visit exchanged clothes and was able thereby to share his term in prison. John married Miss Maclaren, from New Perth, with issue. Henry married but without issue. Both families returned to Andover, Mass. The family claimed to be relations of Martha Carrier, of Andover, who was burned for a witch during the notorious Salem witch trials.

The Enmans of Vernon River

Among the many notable families of Dutch and German origin that remained loyal to Britain during the Revolutionary War in America were the Enmans of Vernon River. Family tradition has it that the first Enman ancestor in the American colonies settled in New York State, that his name was Jeremiah and that he died or was killed in said war. His widow, whose maiden name is said to have been Margaret Benoit, and two sons, Thomas Enman and Jeremiah Enman, migrated to St. John's Island after the war and settled on the south bank of Vernon River. By 1803 they were well established there as appears from Selkirk's diary. The son Thomas Enman settled in the Pownal area, married and had a family, several of whom moved to the Egmont Bay district about 1859. Many descendants live there now, among them Theophilus Enman of Northam, aged 76 in 1955. The headstone in Vernon River churchyard is inscribed as follows: "Sacred to the memory of Jeremiah Enman born in New York 1780 died on P.E. Island Sept. 1857. Also his wife Margaret Fraser born in Scotland Nov 30, 1787 came to P.E. Island 1803. Died Nov. 28, 1864."

Jeremiah Enman and his wife Margaret Fraser had ten children:

Ann Enman, b. May 26, 1805.

Sarah Enman, b. Nov. 1807.

Margaret Enman, b. Feby. 15, 1809.

David Enman, b. July 6, 1811. David Enman married firstly Christene MacLaren (d. July 27, 1866, aged 51), daughter of John MacLaren of Hermitage Grove, Charlottetown Royalty, a Perthshire Scot who had settled on the Island in the early eighteen hundreds. They had eleven children.

John Enman, b. Sept. 5, 1814. John Enman built and operated a mill at Grandview, Murray Harbor Road. He died 1875. His wife was Catherine Wisener, a neighbor. A grandson, Martin Enman, with wife and family reside on the ancestral farm.

Jeremiah Enman II, b. Dec. 25, 1816. Jeremiah Enman II, Vernon River, married Marjory MacLaren (d. Dec. 22, 1902, aged 81), daughter of John MacLaren of Hermitage Grove. Their grandson, Horace Luttrell Enman is President of the Bank of Nova Scotia. The present

Lieutenant Governor of New Brunswick, David Lawrence MacLaren, is great grandson of said John MacLaren.

Isabella Enman, b. April 10, 1820.

Mary Enman, b. March 24, 1823.

Thomas Enman, b. May 27, 1825. Thomas Enman married Frances Benson (d. 1904, aged 76) of England. They had several children, one of whom, Osbert Enman (1860-1952), married Edith Vessey (died 1954 aged 90) of Little York, leaving several children. Their two sons—Warren Enman (b. 1896) married Etta Murchison, daughter of Donald Murchison of Kinross and his wife Miss Compton, with issue; and Roy Enman (b. 1898) married Donaldina Murchison, sister of Etta, with issue—are well known representatives of the family in Vernon River in 1957.

Daniel Enman, b. April 22, 1828.

A detailed genealogical chart of the Enmnan family was filed in the Public Library in Charlottetown in 1956.

Martins of Newtown River

Angus Martin, a descendant of the Martins of Bealach, in Trotternish, Skye, in 1733 held a written tack for certain lands in Glenmore, in the Parish of Portree. He had a son, Peter Martin, of Snizort, Skye, who was married to Margaret

Macaulay, daughter of Rev. Donald Macaulay, M.A., minister of Bracadale, Skye. (Her sister, Alice Macaulay, was wife of Rev. William Macqueen, M.A., minister of Snizort).

Peter Martin and his wife Margaret had a son, Donald, born in Snizort in 1759, who emigrated to Belfast, in 1803, where he died in 1848. His wife was Marion MacLeod, of Applecross (1770-1845). They settled on Newtown River, Belfast. Said Donald had a brother, Martin Martin (1767-1860) tacksman of Shulishadder, now part of Portree. Martin's eldest son, Alexander, was an auctioneer in Portree, where he died, 15 February, 1881, aged 81. Alexander's daughter, Margaret Martin, was wife of Malcolm Campbell, of Portree, and their daughter, Janet Campbell, was wife of Rev. Ewen Macqueen, minister in the City of Inverness. Janet died shortly prior to 1940.

Peter Martin (1809-1877) son of Donald Martin and his wife Marion MacLeod, inherited the homestead on Newtown River. His wife was Sarah Mackinnon, a neighbor. Of their large and talented family a son, Donald Charles Martin (b. 1850, d. 1888), graduated from Dalhousie U., was called to P.E.I. bar in 1879; member of local legislature, 1882-1888, K.C., was unmarried. A younger son, Kenneth John Martin, K.C., B.A., Dalhousie U., called to bar of P.E.I. in 1889; was Stipendiary Magistrate in Charlottetown for many years. He was succeeded in this position by his son, Kenneth Montgomery Martin, K.C., the present incumbent (1957).

Margaret Martin (1806-Nov. 5, 1892) sister of said Peter, was wife of Malcolm Macqueen (February 18, 1804-October 29, 1886) son of Donald Macqueen and his wife Christine Macleod of Glasphein, Skye, both of whom arrived in Belfast, in 1803 and lived near the mouth of Pinette River. After her husband's death about 1812, widow Macqueen and her children moved to Orwell where they bought a hundred acre farm on the north bank of Orwell River. Of the three sons, Malcolm, John and Angus, no descendant of the name resides in the district today except Peter Macqueen, son of John Angus, son of aforesaid Malcolm.

Of the children of Donald Martin and his wife Marion, a daughter, Katherine, married Robert Grant. Among their many descendants is George Grant, insurance agent, Charlottetown. Donald and Marion's son Kenneth Martin married Alice Moore of Union Road, Kings Co. Their son Angus Martin, master mariner, married Mary Ann Hamilton of New Perth, with issue a son, Herbert H. Martin, Ph. D., professor in Drake University and Iowa State U. He died in Tucson, Arizona, in 1953, aged 82. After Capt. Angus Martin was lost at sea his widow married Thomas Mellish, Union

Road. Their son Thomas W. Mellish lives on the ancestral home.

John Martin (1811-1862), son of Donald and Marion Martin, married Emily Compton.

There are many descendants.

Munros of Alberry Plans

A member of the Munro clan, perhaps from Katewell, Easter Ross, settled in Skye at an early date. The Strath Rentals mentions one John Munro as early as 1720. He is described as John Ban Mac Uilleam alias Munro—that is, fair-haired John, son of William Munro. One John Munro appears in 1778; also Andrew Munro, who was probably father of George Munro, "The Miller of Strath," whose wife was Janet Macqueen, believed daughter of James Macqueen of Sleat, writer, who was son of Rev. Angus Macqueen of Sleat, one of whose daughters was wife of Rev. Donald Macaulay, minister of Kilmuir and Bracadale, Skye, to whose family belonged Lord Macaulay. George Munro and his wife, Janet Macqueen, had several children, one of whom was James Munro, already referred to. He studied medicine in Edinburgh U. in 1785 and 1786 and practiced in Skye until 1840. His wife was Annabella MacLeod (1792-1852), daughter of Capt. Murdo MacLeod, tacksman of Cuidrach, Skye (second son of Alexander

MacLeod, in 1781 described in a legal document as "late of Peinmore, now of Camustenavaig"), and his wife Marion Macdonald, daughter of Major Alexander Macdonald, tacksman of Cuidrach, and his wife Annabella Macdonald, half-sister of the celebrated Flora Macdonald of Kingsburgh, the tack adjoining Cuidrach.

Annabella's father was Capt. Hugh Macdonald of Armadale, Skye, son of Somerled Macdonald, of Sartil (1641-1700), son of Sir James Macdonald (d. 1678), Chief of Clan Donald.

George Munro and wife, Janet Macqueen had a son Alexander Munro, born in Skye in 1774. He was a schoolmaster and catechist for the Society for Propagating Christian Knowledge and began teaching in Ferinlea, Bracadale, on May 1, 1821, continuing there until Nov. 1, 1832. He next taught at Shawbost, Parish of Lochs, Lewis, until May 1, 1838, when superannuated. In 1842 he migrated to P.E. Island, settling first in what was known as Brown's Creek, now Valleyfield. Here he taught school and helped organize a church. Later he settled in Lorne Valley. In this newly occupied district he was a leader. He conducted religious services there and in Dundas. He was buried in Brown's Creek Cemetery.

One of the family of said Alexander Munro was Thomas Boston Munro, born at Triaslan, Skye, Oct. 17, 1817; taught school at Shawbost, in 1838; sailed from Loch Uig, Skye, July 14, 1840 in the brig *Ruther*, arriving in Charlottetown Sept. 8, 1840. He settled in Lorne Valley. His wife was Sarah Shaw (b. Oct. 17, 1825, d. June 3, 1888) of Pinette. Thomas Boston Munro had four sons and four daughters. All migrated to Nebraska in 1874. A son Alexander Munro, Ph.D., finally settled in N.Y. City, where he was one of the inspectors of schools. He married and had a son Thomas Munro, Ph.D., born Omaha, 1897, professor in Columbia U., Rutgers U. and Western Reserve U. Married with issue, a son and two daughters. George A. Munro, another son of Thomas Boston Munro was a Congregational minister. Dr. James Munro and Alexander Munro had at least two brothers, Andrew and John. The latter lived in Grantown, Inverness, in 1842. His son Andrew was a soldier in Capetown. There were also sons Kenneth and Donald. Thomas Boston Munro, had a brother John, who lived in Lorne Valley, married, with several children; also twin sisters, Ann and Mary Munro, born April 1, 1832 at Shawbost, Parish of Lochs, Lewis. Mary married Allan MacSwain, a master mariner, of Lorne Valley, in 1865. He was lost at sea. Mary passed away on March 5, 1937, without issue, aged almost 106.

Nicholson of Orwell Cove and Orwell River

1. Rev. Donald Nicolson, M.A., twelfth chief of Scorrybreac, in Skye, was a notable man in his day. He was Episcopal minister of Kilmuir from 1663 to 1696 and died in 1697. Owing to his zeal for Episcopacy he relinquished his charge rather than conform to Presbyterianism. Few records in the Church of Scotland equal that of Rev. Donald Nicolson, for thirty-two of his descendants have been ministers. He was married three times and left twenty-three, or as some say, twenty-five children. Seventeen of these were by his third wife, Margaret, daughter of Rev. Kenneth Morrison of Stornoway. Three of his sons were ministers: Rev. Malcolm, M.A., died young; Rev. Patrick, was minister of Kiltarlity; and Rev. Alexander was Episcopal minister of Steinshole in 1715.
2. Donald Nicolson, tacksman of Tall-na-ta-in, Upper Uig, in 1735, was son of Rev. Donald and from him the Orwell Nicholsons are believed to be descended. He was dead by 1748 leaving three sons, Donald, Peter and Malcolm.
3. Malcolm Nicolson, described in 1771, as tacksman of Steinshole.
4. Donald.
5. John, known locally as Steinshole, emigrated from Staffin, Skye and settled in Orwell Cove,

beside Newtown River, in 1803.

6. DONALD NICHOLSON, one of the sons of said John, received a grant from Selkirk of the 200 acre farm on both banks of Orwell River. He returned to Skye in 1804, where he married Isabel Nicholson. In 1805 or 1806 he was back in Orwell and settled on his homestead. He built the first mill on Orwell River. Selkirk refers to him as "the leading man of the Skye party," calling him Steinshole.

7. His son PETER, (1809-1884), known locally as Patrick Steinshole, married Marion (1812-1897) daughter of Dr. James Munro (Edin. U. 1785-86) of Uig, Skye. Two sons and a daughter died in infancy but three daughters survived:

A. ISABELLA (5 February 1845-3 July 1926), wife of John Angus Macqueen (March 10, 1836-May 25, 1918), son of Malcolm Macqueen of Orwell (b. February 18, 1804, d. Oct 29, 1886) and his wife Margaret Martin of Newtown (b. 1806, d. Nov. 5, 1892, married February 2, 1830), son of Donald Macqueen (and his wife Christina MacLeod, of Glasphein, near Staffin, Skye), emigrants of 1803, who settled on Orwell River; with issue surviving in 1957:

(1) Matilda Brown, b. March 17, 1877, wife of Walter David Ross (1875-1941) of Kinross, with issue:

(a) David Douglas (b. March 24, 1913; B. Com., U. of T., C.A.), company executive, Arnprior, Ont.; Lt. Col. World War II, O. C. Unit in England; married Sheila Hope Price, daughter of Harry Price of Quebec City, with issue:
   (i) Barbara Jane (b. Jan'y 16, 1948).
   (ii) Daphne Isobel (b. June 3, 1947).
   (iii) Pamela Muriel (b. February 18, 1950).
(b) Marion Isabel (b. 1916, B.A., Dal. U.; Boston U.), wife of Alexander Beaton of Milton, Mass.
(2) Malcolm A. (b. Dec. 8, 1878, B.A., Queen's U.) barrister, Winnipeg, married Harriet Murgatroyd Riley, Winnipeg.
(3) Peter Isaac (b. Dec. 15, 1880), Orwell, married Belle Irene.

B. ELIZABETH (1850-1923), wife of Alexander William MacLeod (d. 1919), master mariner, of Orwell Cove, of the MacLeods of Kilmaluag, Skye, with issue surviving:
(1) William, retired railway employee, Colorado, m. secondly, Alma Taylor of Texas, with issue surviving:
   (a) Ruth, married Mr. Klein of Sugar City, Colorado, with issue:
      (i) John.
      (ii) David.

(iii) Karen.

(2) Mary, m. firstly, George Mutch, of Earnscliffe, P.E.I., with issue:

(a) Benjamin, m. with issue:

(i) Sallie.

Mary m. secondly, Harold B. Collins (B.Sc., U. of Alberta), lumber company executive, Vancouver, B.C.

(3) Marion, wife of Rodger Cronsberry, civil service, Ottawa, with issue:

(a) Alexander, Flight Lieut. R.C.A.F., Ottawa, m. Flora Richardson, with issue, with two daughters.

(i) Kent Alexander.

(b) Alice.

(c) Marion Eliza, wife of Leonard Turner, civil service, Ottawa.

(d) Eleanor Elizabeth, Lieut. In C.W.A.C., wife of Mr. Murphy, civil service, Ottawa, two daughters.

C. ANNABELLA (d. Nov. 12, 1939) wife of Daniel Nicholson (b. Union Road, P.E.I., 1850, d. Victoria, B.C., 1931), with issue:

(1) Sarah Louise, Victoria, B.C.

(2) Arthur Stirling, (Sept. 28, 1884-May 5, 1949), Phoenix, Arizona, married Myrtle Singer, of Spokane, with issue:

(a) Gordon Daniel (b. 1910), Stanford U.; Capt. in U.S. Army, World War II.

(3) Ruth, (b. 1899), wife of Arthur A. Dods (a relation of Rev. Marcus Dods, Edinburgh, Scottish divine), Victoria, B.C., with issue:
(a) Gordon Arthur (1929), U. of B.C., Geological Engineer.
(b) Marion, (1933), married May 4, 1957, Duard Daniel Ball of McAlester, Oklahoma, Lieut. in U. S. Army.

Mr. and Mrs. Daniel Nicholson migrated to Monrovia, Calif. in 1887 and two years later to Phoenix, Arizona, where they prospered in business.

Hannah Nicholson (d. 1881, about 75) was sister of aforesaid Peter Nicholson. She married William Harris, millwright, born in Bideford, Devon, England, who died at Milton, P.E.I. in 1884, aged 80. Their daughter, Janet Harris (d. 1904, aged 68), was wife of Thomas Darke, born in Bideford, who died at Milton, in 1884, aged 59. Among their children was Francis Nicholson Darke (b. Oct. 26, 1863), M.P. Regina.

Descendants of Rev. William Macqueen in Orwell

In his great work, *The Surnames of Scotland, Their Origin, History and Meaning,* George Black, Ph.D., for many years of the New York Public Library, holds that the Skye surname Macqueen is of Norse origin from the personal name Sveinn. There is also a tradition that the Macqueens of Skye are descendants of the Macqueen who formed part of the living *tocher* sent from Ireland before 1330, by the Ulster baron Conn O'Cathan with his daughter Lady Margaret when she married Angus Og of Isla, Lord of the Isles, Bruce's lieutenant at Bannockburn. Rev. Dr. Donald Mackinnon, historian of Skye, in an article in *The MacLeod Magazine* for 1948-49 and 1950 develops this theory. Whatever their origin, the Macqueens of Skye have had a long ecclesiastical history, having given an aggregate of over five hundred years in the ministerial service of the church, a record perhaps unsurpassed by any Highland or Island family.

Dr. Mackinnon names Angus Mor Macqueen, a famous drover in his day, as first of the name in Rigg, Skye. He married Jane, daughter of Donald Dubb Cameron of Locheil.

The first cleric in the family seems to have been:

1. REV. EWEN MACQUEEN. He was minister of Rodil, Harris before 26 March, 1604, and was minister in Duirnish in 1614. He died about 1643. He had two sons ministers, viz. Rev. Angus and Rev. Archibald.
2. REV. ARCHIBALD MACQUEEN, graduated M.A. from Glasgow U. in 1636, and was appointed minister of Snizort, in or about 1642. In 1659

he was minister of Kilmuir, but was minister in Snizort in 1660. He died in 1684.

3. REV. DONALD MACQUEEN, graduated M.A., from Edinburgh U. on July 27, 1663 and succeeded his father as minister of Snizort. He was archdeacon of the Isles under the Episcopal regime. After the Revolution he was deprived of his parish for refusing to conform to Presbyterianism. He was still living in Rigg in 1710. His wife was Margaret, daughter of Hugh Macdonald of Glenmore, second son of Sir James Macdonald, second baronet of Sleat. They had a son Archibald.

4. REV. ARCHIBALD MACQUEEN, M.A., (1671-Sept. 24, 1754), was graduated M.A. Edinburgh U. on 6 July 1699, and was ordained on March 17, 1706. He was minister of Snizort from 1706 to 1753. The "Fasti" records that he "was a person of uncommon abilities and distinguished himself as well by his erudition and extensive knowledge, as by his piety, zeal and other virtues." By his first wife, Isobell Mackenzie, daughter of Alexander Mackenzie III of Applecross, he had a son Rev. Donald Macqueen, M.A., minister of Kilmuir, Skye, from 1740 to 1785, who won the respect of Dr. Johnson for his learning. By his second wife, Florence, daughter of William, "The Tutor" of Sleat, third son of Sir Donald Macdonald,

chief, whom he married October 3, 1719, he had among others, a son William.

5. REV. WILLIAM MACQUEEN (1720-17 Sept. 1787) graduated M.A. Edinburgh U., licensed by presbytery of Skye, 3rd Sept. 1746, became minister of Snizort on 11 April 1753, in succession to his father. Son succeeded father for four generations in this parish. It is said he was an excellent classical scholar, versed in all branches of learning, and greatly beloved by his parishioners. He married his second cousin Alice (d. July 15, 1785), daughter of Rev. Donald Macaulay (1674-1748, M.A., Edin. U. 1692), minister of Bracadale and Kilmuir, who was married to Catherine, daughter of Rev. Angus Macqueen, second son of Rev. Archibald Macqueen, minister of Sleat. Rev. William and Alice had seven sons and three daughters. Rev. Donald Macaulay was first cousin of Rev. Aulay Macaulay of Harris, ancestor of Lord Macaulay. Of the ten children of Rev. William, one was:

6. CATHERINE MACQUEEN, wife of Alexander Macleod, tacksman of Peinmore and later of Camustinavaig, Parish of Portree, Skye. Their first son, John, was born in 1769; their second son was Murdo. Said Alexander may have been son of Murdo, son of Norman of Cuidrach, son of Murdo of Raasay, styled "The Tutor," son of Alexander Macleod, IV of Raasay.

An Assignment in writing, dated December 31st, 1781, of Bond dated 28th June, 1771, recites as follows:

I, Alexander Macleod, late in Peinmore, now of Camustinavaig, for the love, favour and affection which I have and bear to Murdoch McLeod my second son and other considerations do hereby make and constitute the said Murdoch McLeod, his heirs and Donators my Cessioners and Assignees in and to the sum of two thousand merks Scots money of principal with the sum of four hundred merks like money of liquidate expences ... in a bond granted to me by the Right Honourable Alexander Macdonald of Macdonald, Baronet, dated the twenty-eighth day of June seventeen hundred and seventy one years ... Dated 31st December, 1781, and intimated 19 October 1782.

(Above from Macdonald Charter Chest through courtesy of Mr. James Macintyre, author of *Castles of Skye*, now factor to Col. Stirling, Tower of Fairburn, Muir of Ord, Rossshire, but former assistant to Mr. George M. Fraser, factor to Lord Macdonald, Portree)

7. CAPT. MURDO MACLEOD was married to Marion, daughter of Major Alexander Macdonald, tacksman of Cuidrach (adjoining Kingsburgh) and his wife Annabella, daughter of Capt. Hugh Macdonald of Armadale (son of Somerled Macdonald of Sartil (1641-1700) son of Sir James Macdonald (d. Dec. 8, 1678), chief of Clan Donald, and his wife Marion Macdonald, mother by her first husband of the celebrated Flora Macdonald.

Murdo was alive in 1826 for he appeared on a bond dated October 26, 1826, as one of the trustees of the estate of his brother-in-law, Major Alexander Macdonald of Courthill, Loch Carron, as lending Lord Macdonald five hundred pounds. (Alexander and Murdo were married to the sisters Janet and Marion Macdonald.) He was dead by 1829 for the tack was renewed from Whitsunday, 1829, to Arthur Stewart, who succeeded "Murdo Macleod's heirs" in the tenancy.

Murdo Macleod may be regarded as a typical member of the tacksman class to which he belonged. Being a man of means he employed tutors for his daughters. These were usually students of Divinity. One of them, Alexander Macleod, and Murdoch's daughter, Margaret, fell in love, but the impecunious student was considered an unsuitable match for the proud tacksman's daughter. However, as sometimes happens, they eloped, were pursued by the outraged tacksman but were married before he overtook them. Not until he became minister of one of the leading churches in Lewis was Alexander forgiven for his act of presumption. In later life he was minister of the Free Church in Rogart. From there until about 1870, Margaret and her sister Annabella Munro maintained a frequent correspondence. Margaret and Rev. Alexander had no children.

Captain Murdo and Marion had six children, one of them:

8. ANNABELLA MACLEOD (died Alberry Plains, P.E. Island, August 1852, aged 60), wife of James Munro (son of George Munro, the "Miller of Strath" and his wife Janet Macqueen), who studied medicine in Edinburgh University in 1785-1786. Thereafter he practiced his profession in Uig, Skye, until 1840 when with his wife, three sons and four daughters, his brother Alexander, cathechist and schoolmaster, and family he sailed on the brig *Ruther*, 247 tons of Sunderland, for P.E. Island. Stricken with pneumonia he was put ashore at Tobermory, with wife and two youngest daughters. There he died.

9. MARION MUNRO (1812-June 1897) daughter of Dr. James Munro, was wife of Peter Nicholson

(1809-1884), son of Donald Nicholson, with issue reaching maturity three daughters, Isabella, Elizabeth and Annabella.

Rev. William Macqueen had a son Kenneth who engaged in mercantile pursuits in Calcutta, where he died. In his will dated Nov. 22, 1805, he named his distant cousin Doctor Malcolm Macqueen of Ridgmont, near Woburn, Bedfordshire, England, his sole executor. The Supreme Court of Judicature at Fort William in Bengal, granted administration to William Blackston, Registrar of said Court on August 29, 1811. This Will was admitted to probate at Somerset House, London, on March 14, 1812 and administration granted to Dr. Malcolm Macqueen. On November 15, 1872, administration of the goods unadministered was granted to Alice (daughter of Rev. James Macqueen, brother of Kenneth, and minister of North Uist), widow of Alexander MacLean of Hosts, Capt. in 79 Cameron Highlanders.

In 1874 Margaret Macintyre (only child of Hugh Macintyre, a Skyeman who prospered in mercantile business in London, and his wife Marion, d. of Capt. Murdo Macleod of Cuidrach), second wife of Rev. George Rainy Kennedy, minister of Dornoch, was appointed administratrix Quoad Non Executa, of the late Capt. Macleod, to recover the share to which his representatives were entitled of the residue of the late Kenneth Macqueen, of Calcutta.

In the final distribution made through A. Leslie of Dornoch, the children of Dr. James Munro and his wife Annabella Macleod, then both deceased, were adjudged entitled to one half the residue of £1131-10-6; same was paid in 1878 through Palmer and MacLeod, barristers, Charlottetown.

PETER ALEXANDER MACQUEEN OF TOWNSVILLE, AUSTRALIA

The above was born in Orwell, P.E. Island, March 26, 1842, son of Malcolm Macqueen (1804-1886) and his wife Margaret Martin (1806-1892) of Newtown. Malcolm was son of Donald Macqueen and his wife Christy MacLeod of Glasphein, Skye, who came to P.E.I. in 1803. After teaching school for a few years Peter went to Australia, about 1867. There he married Elizabeth Marshall Neilsen (d. May 14, 1931) d. of James Neilsen. Peter died in Townsville, August, 1938. Their issue:

    A. PETER ANGUS, deceased, m. Ethel Cruckshank, of Townsville, with issue:
        1. Cedric Norman.
        2. Leslie Angus.
        3. Malcolm Frederick.
        4. Elizabeth.

5. Ethlyn.
6. Dulcie.
7. Enid.
B. JESSIE MARSHALL (b. 18th November, 1878) Townsville, unmarried. Living in April, 1957.
C. ISABELL BURT (b. May 9, 1880), wife of Cleveland Cruckshank, Townsville, (d. April 10, 1931, aged 48). Living in April, 1957, with issue.
1. Jessamine Isabell, died age 5.
2. Reginald Cleveland (b. July 6, 1911), foreman N. Q. Ry. Co., m. Rita Rosendahl.
3. Nancy Leila (b. Dec. 1913), wife of Arthur Robert Conn, merchant, Hughenden, with issue:
(a) Robert (b. 1944).
(b) Iris (b. 1948).
4. Leslie Orwell (b. Dec. 21, 1915), m. Kathleen Millwood of Tasmania, residing in Tully, with issue:
(a) Ronald Orwell (b. March 21, 1943).
(b) Leslie George (b. March 17, 1945).
5. Ronald Harry (b. January 27, 1921). In Australian Army in Malaya, World War II. Prisoner of War in Singapore for over three years.
D. MALCOLM TOWERS, Aus. Army World War I; in Dardanelles and Flanders. Died in

Australia from effects of wounds received in Flanders; unmarried.

E. ORWELL, Aus. Army World War I; in Dardanelles and Flanders. Killed in action in Flanders; unmarried.

F. LEILA, wife of Stephen Cumming Anning, sugar planter, Cornelia, Q'land, without issue. Living in April, 1957.

G. ADELAIDE, married Frederick Dalgleish Lodge, in June, 1938; d. May 17, 1948; without issue.

DR. MALCOLM MACQUEEN AND COL. THOMAS POTTER MACQUEEN, M.P. OF BEDFORDSHIRE, ENGLAND

Although having no direct connection with Belfast, Dr. Macqueen and his son, Col. Potter Macqueen, M.P., had many relatives there, and as their history is of interest to some of these collaterals, the following record, compiled by Rev. Dr. Donald Mackinnon, is introduced:

1. ANGUS MOR MACQUEEN of Rigg, in his day a famous drover, had a son Ewen.
2. REV. EWEN MACQUEEN was minister of Harris and of Duirinish from 1626 to 1660.
3. KENNETH MACQUEEN, progenitor of the Macqueens of Totaroam, 1663, was one of his sons.

4. His son, KENNETH OG MACQUEEN, 1697, married Christine, daughter of Murdoch Matheson of Balmacara, Localsh. Among their children were: Angus Macqueen of Totaroam, Lauchlan of Flodigarry and John.
5. ANGUS MACQUEEN of Totaroam, married Jane, daughter of Alexander Mackenzie of Applecross. They had issue, Archibald; Mary, who married Dr. Alexander Nicolson of Sleat, with issue; Catherine, who married Malcolm Macleod of Brae, Raasay; Jane, who married John Macleod, of Raasay, the entertainer of Boswell and Johnson; also Janet.
6. ARCHIBALD MACQUEEN, son of Angus, was a lieutenant in the Macdonald Independent Company, commanded by Capt. Hugh Macdonald, of Armadale. In the flight of Prince Charlie, after Culloden, he helped procure a boat to ferry the Prince from Portree to Raasay. He was married to his first cousin, Flora Macleod, of Raasay, daughter of Malcolm Macleod, laird of Raasay, and sister of John MacLeod, laird of Raasay. This marriage took place in 1746 or earlier. Archibald predeceased his father, having died between 1747 and 1757, in which year his widow Flora, married, as second husband, Donald Nicolson tacksman of Monkstadt, Kilmuir. Nicolson died in 1761, leaving issue. Flora then married her third husband, Roderick

Macdonald, of Sleat and of Sandaig, Glenelg, with issue Alexander and Flora.

7. MALCOLM MACQUEEN, son of Archibald and his wife Flora, was born in or about 1746. As his father died while Malcolm was still a child, his father's first cousin Rev. Donald Macqueen, minister of Kilmuir, companion of Boswell and Johnson on their tour in Skye, was appointed his "tutor" or guardian. Their relationship arose thus: Angus Macqueen of Totaroam, Rev. Archibald Macqueen, minister of Snizort, and Malcolm Macleod, laird of Raasay, were all married to daughters of Alexander Mackenzie of Applecross. Thus Archibald Macqueen of Totaroam, Rev. Donald Macqueen of Kilmuir, and John Macleod, laird of Raasay, were first cousins. Archibald married his first cousin, Flora Macleod, of Raasay and John Macleod of Raasay married his first cousin, Jane Macqueen of Totaroam. When Doctor Johnson and Boswell were being entertained at Raasay in 1773, Boswell mentions among the guests "Rorie Macdonald in Sandaig ... and his wife, sister of Raasay's ... as also—Macqueen, son of Rorie's wife by the first marriage, who was going to America." It does not appear that Malcolm went to America, for in January of the following year he appears as a doctor on the Macleod estates and remained there

until Whitsuntide, 1776. After this he went to England where he practiced his profession at Ridgmont, near Woburn, Bedfordshire. He succeeded to the manor of Bevane, in Segenhoe parish. He died in 1829. In his Last Will, dated 19 June, 1829, and proved in the Prerogative Court of Canterbury, by Thomas Potter Macqueen, Esq., "the son and sole executor," the Doctor left "to my maternal sister Flora Macdonald residing now in the Isle of Skye, Scotland £60 per ann. for her life."

Malcolm Macqueen, M.D. married Maria Potter, one of the two daughters of Thomas Potter (1718-1759) and his second wife, Miss Lowe, of Brightwell, Oxfordshire. Thomas was the second son of John Potter (1674?-1747), Archbishop of Canterbury. The Archbishop disinherited his eldest son John, because he had married a domestic servant, and left his fortune to Thomas, whose wife also possessed £50,000 and the estate of Ridgmont, near Woburn, Bedfordshire. The joint fortunes and estates of Thomas and his wife eventually passed to Malcolm Macqueen.

Thomas Potter was M.P. for Aylesbury Borough (Buckinghamshire) from 1754 to 1757, and for Oakhampton Borough (Devonshire) from 1757 to 1759, in which year he died at Ridgmont.

Dr. Malcolm Macqueen and his wife, Maria

Potter, had among other children, an elder son Col. Thomas Potter Macqueen, who served in early life in a cavalry regiment, but afterwards commanded the Bedfordshire Yeomanry Cavalry; also a son Captain John Macqueen, Life Guards, who received his first commission from King George IV.

Thomas Potter Macqueen was member of Parliament for East Looe Borough (Cornwall) from 1816 to 1826, and for Bedford County from 1826 to 1830. In the Return of Members of Parliament he is described, during the period 1816-1826 as "of Ridgmont House, County Bedford."

In May 1824, he received from the crown a grant of 20,000 acres of land near the junction of the Page and Hunter Rivers in New South Wales, Australia (West of Newcastle). In November of the same year two ships loaded with emigrants and equipped with stock and general stores, under the management of Peter Macintyre, Potter Macqueen's agent, and his assistant, Alexander Campbell, set out to pioneer this grant. The ships arrived in Sydney in April, 1825. A pretentious home, still standing, was erected. The estate was named Segenhoe. Macqueen made several voyages to Australia and in 1840 published a volume "Australia as She Is and May Be."

In his last will dated 23rd January, 1853, Thomas Potter Macqueen is described as of Oswestry in the county of Salop, Esquire. In it he appoints his son-in-law John Long Marshall, Esquire, and his friend George Edwards of Stroud in the county of Gloucester, Gentlemen, executors and trustees.

On the 22nd March, 1856, administration (with the will annexed) was granted to James Wingfield, attorney of John Phillips Beavan, Esquire, a creditor, the executors having renounced, by the Prerogative Court of Canterbury (folio 226). This Court was abolished by the Probate Act, and the Probate Court was set up in 1857. The Probate Court of Canterbury is housed in the Principal Probate Registry, Somerset House.

The will and grant of administration refer to his two daughters Flora Georgina Macqueen, spinster, and Anne Burgess Marshall, and to his son Henry Archibald Potter Macqueen, to whom he willed his estate equally. He explained that he left nothing to his eldest son, John Potter Macqueen, because he was already provided for from the proceeds of the sale of his Bedfordshire estates. John was captain in the Army in 1834 and served in the Life Guards. In 1873 he was proprietor of Radwell Moor End. His name disappears from the register of electors and jurors after 1876-7.

The *Gentleman's Magazine* carried the following reference to Henry: Dec. 28, 1857. At Kimedy, Madras, aged 26, Lt. Henry Archibald Potter Macqueen, 31st Regt. youngest son of late Col. Potter

Macqueen, M.P. for Bedford and nephew of Rt. Hon. Lord Hastings of Melton Constable, Norfolk and Seaton De Laval, Northumberland.

Robertsons and Fergusons of Marshfield, P.E.I.

The recorded ancestor of the Robertsons of Marshfield, Prince Edward Island, known to that branch of the family, is James (?) Robertson, who flourished in Blair Atholl, Perthshire, Scotland, between 1750 and 1800. He was married and had issue, among others, James and Margaret, both of whom emigrated to P.E. Island.

    A. JAMES ROBERTSON (1770-1842) married Jean Miller. They lived in the city of Perth, where all their children were born. In 1818 they emigrated to P.E.I. They had issue, among others:

        1. ALEXANDER ROBERTSON (1800-1875) married his first cousin Margaret Fergusson, with issue, among others:

            a. Alexander (1842-1910), married his first cousin, Emma Vickerson, with issue, among others:

                (i) Lemuel Fergus (M.A., McGill; LL.D., U. of B.C.), Dean of Arts, U. of B.C.; (d. May 14, 1956), married Floretta, d. of Norman Macleod, Orwell,

P.E.I. and Vancouver, and his wife Mary Ann MacSwain, sister of Dr. Angus MacSwain, with issue:

(1a) Norman Robertson, b. 1904 (M.A., U. of B.C.), Canadian High Commissioner in London, and Canadian Ambassador in Washington, 1957, married H. J. Welling, of Holland, with issue:
1. Flora Johanna, b. March 8, 1931.
2. Judith Alida, b. April 29, 1942.

(2a) Mary (B.A., U. of B. C), wife of John Oliver (C.E., U. of B.C.), Vancouver, with issue:
1. Craig Robertson (M.A., Queens U.), b. August 31, 1931.
2. Peter Fergus, b. April 11, 1935.

(3a) Barbara (B.A., U. of B.C.), wife of H. W. Morton (Ph. D.), Ottawa, with issue:
1. Brian Christopher, b. February 2, 1942.

(ii) William, barrister, Calgary, married.

(iii) Charles, of Chilliwack, B.C., married Elizabeth Smith, daughter of Jeremiah Smith, of Newtown, P.E.I., without issue.

2. Jessie Robertson (1802-1875) wife of Conrad Vickerson, son of a cornet in the Hessian army in the Revolutionary War (1776-1782) and his wife, Catherine Borsner, also Hessian with issue:
  a. Emma (1842-1888), wife of her first cousin, Alexander Robertson, with issue.
B. Margaret Robertson was wife of John Fergusson (1772-1840). Some of their children were born in Blair Atholl, Perthshire, but one at least, Margaret Ferguson, (1809-1893), was born on P.E.I., to which they emigrated in 1808. She became wife of her first cousin, Alexander Robertson, who also was born on the Island.

John Fergusson and his wife, Margaret Robertson of Marshfield, P.E.I., had, among other issue, a son, Donald Ferguson (the spelling he adopted), born in Marshfield, P.E.I., in 1839. He was a successful breeder of purebred cattle. Called to the senate he became leader of the Conservative party in that venerable chamber. His wife was Elizabeth Scott. They left several children, among whom Colin Campbell Ferguson and William Ferguson were McGill graduates; the former was actuary and general manager of The Great West Life Assurance Company, Winnipeg; the latter professor of history at Harvard.

Tweedy and Irving Families

The Tweedy family appeared for the first time in Cherry Valley and Vernon River, with the arrival of four brothers and two sisters from Yorkshire, England, where the family had an ancient lineage. A branch flourished at Driffield, East Riding, in 1818. The ancestors of those who settled on P.E. Island were brewers. Largely owing to their advanced standards in education and farming methods the Tweedies upheld the high standards of Yorkshire men generally and made excellent pioneers.

A. JOHN TWEEDY, unmarried.
B. GEORGE TWEEDY, married twice, with issue, George, of North River, married with issue, a daughter residing in Charlottetown.
C. THOMAS TWEEDY, married Sarah Furness, a sister of John and Thomas Furness, of Vernon River Bridge, with issue:
   1. THOMAS, of Eldon, unmarried.
   2. CEPHAS BARKER, Vernon River, married Charlotte McMillan, a neighbor, with issue:
      a. Weldon, unmarried.
      b. George Joseph, Justice of the Supreme Court of P.E.I., married Miss Mackenzie, with issue.

c. Irving, married Miss Sheidow.
3. GEORGE, M.D., (U. of Toronto), Winona, Minnesota, died July 20, 1951, aged 90, married with issue, two sons, Robert and John, both physicians in Winona.
4. ANNE, wife of David P. Irving, M.L.A., Vernon River Bridge, whose ancestors came from Dumfries, Scotland; with issue, a distinguished family of six sons and six daughters. Six or seven were graduates of McGill U. One of them, Thomas Tweedy Irving (B.A.Sc.) was Regional Chief Engineer, Canadian National Railway, Toronto Division, until retirement a few years ago.
   5. ELIZABETH, wife of Charles Machon, Murray Harbor, with issue, Mrs. Hawkins.
   6. PENELOPE, unmarried.
D. JOSEPH TWEEDY, Ernscliffe, married Miss Vickerson, with issue:
   1. HARRY, Ernscliffe, married Lou Matheson, Vernon River, with issue, among them two married sons.
   2. ANNE, wife of John Hayden, without issue.
E. ANNE, wife of James Hayden, Ernscliffe, with issue:
   1. JOHN, married Miss Macleod, with issue Lewis, Cherry Valley.
   2. MARY.
F. A brother, a barrister, remained in England,

but his son George and wife, emigrated to P.E.I. After living for a time at North River, he settled in Charlottetown. A tablet in St. Peter's Cathedral, Charlottetown, records his memory.

Index of Names

Settlers, their ancestors, siblings, spouses and descendants.

Acorn. *See also* Eacharn
    Earchern
  Eleanor 164
  Everett 164
  John 160, 164. *See also* John
    Eacharn
  Mathias 164
  Seaforth 164
Angus Mor 30. *See* Big Angus
    MacLeod
Anning
  Stephen Cumming 190
Arbuckle
  Neil 53
Auld
  Elizabeth (nee Hayden) 161

Bagnall
  George 21
Ball
  Duard Daniel 180
Barr
  Angus 144
Beaton
  Alexander 178
  Angus 16, 17, 144
  Donald 144
  John 144
  Saml. 144
Beer
  Joseph 158, 161
  Mathilde 166
Beers. *See also* Beer
  Joseph 157, 158

Bell
  Angus 82
  Dugald 144
  John 144
  Malcolm 144
Benoit
  Margaret 168
Benson
  Frances 170
Bethune
  William 126
Betton
  John 3
Birnie
  George 152, 154
Birt
  Adelaid 146
Blue
  Archibald 144
Borsner
  Catherine 198
Brant
  Joseph 159
Brehaut. *See* Burho
  George Hammond 73
  Louis 73
Bremner
  W. 154
Breuer
  Carl 77
  Catherine 77
Brown
  Angus 120
  Ira M. 152

Matilda 64, 177
Browne
  Robert 11
Browning
  Dorothy Anne 146
Bruce
  Christina 30. *See also* John
    Carrier
  Christine 167
Buchanan
  Donald 144
  John 144
  Malcolm 144
  Murdoch 144
  Samuel 117
Burho. *See* Brehaut
  John 157, 163
Burland
  Georgina 77, *married* John
    Andrew Macphail
Butler
  John 159

Cameron
  Alex. 116
  Alexander 68
  Donald Dubh 181
  Ewen 68
  Jane 181
  Jessie 68
  Roderick 68, 116
Campbell
  Alex. A. 118
  Alexander 194
  Allan A. 119
  Angus (Lieut.) 49
  Arnold Munro 70
  Hector A. 119
  Hiram 48
  Janet 171
  Jessie 67

John 144
Leonard M. 48
Malcolm 75, 171
Mary 64
Neil 118
Norman 119
Peter 144
Robert 49
Roderick A. 118
Roderick 64
Sarah 75
Carlton
  Guy 158
Carrier
  George 167
  Henry 167
  John 30, 167
  Martha 168
  Peter 167
  Stephen 167
Carver
  James 157
Cavanagh
  John 166
Chappell
  Benjamin 21
  F. J. 163
  Theophilus 21
Cheney (early settler) 14
Chisholm
  Michael 74
Clark
  Robert 160
Coles
  G. 154
Collins
  Harold B. 179
Colville
  Andrew 81, 97
Compton
  Emily 173

Conn
  Arthur Robert 189
Costin
  John 157
Coughlin
  Geo. 158
Courie
  James 144
Crane
  Spencer 157
Cronsberry
  Alexander 179
  Alice 179
  Eleanor Elizabeth 179
  Kent Alexander 179
  Marion Eliza 179
  Rodger 179
Cruckshank
  Cleveland 189
  Ethel 188
  Jessamine Isabell 189
  Leslie George 189
  Leslie Orwell 189
  Nancy Leila 189
  Reginald Cleveland 189
  Ronald Harry 189
  Ronald Orwell 189
Cundall
  W. 154
Currie
  Jas. 144
Curtis
  Gill 98

Darby (Captain) 18
Darke
  Francis Nicholson 180
  Thomas 180
Davies
  Benjamin 109
  Daniel 117
  Louis H. 110
  Nathan 109
Davis
  J., Jr. 154
de Jersey 164
Delbridge
  L. M. 77
  Marion 77
Des Barres
  Joseph Frederic Wallet 134
Dixon
  Alexander 98, 99
  Jessie 99
  Joseph 99
  Maclean 99
Dockerty. *See* Odochardy
  Cyrus 146
  John Malcolm, Jr. 146
  John Stewart Mills 146
  Malcolm Birt 146
  Robert 146
Dods
  Arthur A. 180
  Gordon Arthur 180
  Marcus 180
  Marion 180
Dogherty
  K. 154
Douse
  W. 154
  William 101
  Wm. 155
Doyle
  Patrick 53
Drummond
  William 152
Dunham
  Melvin A. 166

Eacharn. *See also* Acorn, Eachern

John 157
Mathias 164
Eachern. *See also* Acorn, Eacharn
 John 164
Edwards
 George 195
Eichorn. *See* Eacharn, Eichern, Acorn
Enman
 Ann 169
 Daniel 170
 David 169
 Horace Luttrell 169
 Isabella 170
 Jeremiah 168, 169
 John 169
 Margaret 169
 Marjory 73
 Martin 169
 Mary 170
 Osbert 170
 Roy 170
 Sarah 169
 Theophilus 169
 Thomas 168, 170
 Warren 170
Enman (widow), *married* James Laird
Evans
 Ernest Charles 88

Ferguson
 Colin Campbell 198
 Donald 198
 Margaret 198
 William 198

Fergusson
 John 198
 Margaret 196

Finlayson
 Allan 119
 Archibald 120
 Kenneth 116
 Murdoch 120
 R. 154
 William 116
Ford
 Miss, *married* John A. Gordon
Fletcher
 James Hayden 75
 James H. 59
 John 75, 95
 Pope 76
Fraser
 Angus 97
 Donald 71
 Isabel 71
 Margaret 169
Fraser (Loyalist) 12
Furness
 John 199
 Robert 162
 Sarah 199
 Thomas 199

Gall
 L.W. 154
Gay
 Ephraim 166
 George 95
 Henry 166
 John 95, 166
 Thankful 166
Gilles
 John 144
Gillies
 John 144
Gillis
 Donald 143
 Gamaliel 28

John 117, 120
Malcolm 28, 30
Murdoch 143
Goodwin
  Maud 63
Gordon
  Alex M. 86
  Alvin H. 72
  Daniel Miner 86
  John A. 72
  John P. 72
  Peter 72
Graham
  Donald 53
Grant
  George 172
  Matthew 2
  Robert 172
Griffin
  Patrick 53
Griffiths
  D. Lloyd 88

Hadin. *See* Hayden
Haley
  John 158
Hamilton
  Mary Ann 172
Harris
  Janet 180
  William 180
Hartz (mason) 15
Hassard
  William 157
Haviland
  T. H. 154
Hayden
  Alex. Lewis 160
  Ann 160, 162
  Caroline 75
  Catherine 160, 162
  Charlotte P. 162
  Cuthbert 163
  Elizabeth 160, 161
  Frederick 160
  Geo. 157
  George 160, 161
  Jacob Lewis 160
  James 75, 160, 162, 163, 200
  James Lewis 96, 159, 161
  James L. 157, 159, 161
  J. L. 161
  John 161, 200
  Lemuel 163
  Lemuel Cambridge 162
  Lemuel C. 163
  Margaret 158, 160, 161
  Maria 160, 162
  Mary 200
  Mary B. 162
  Sidney 162
  William 160
Heathwood
  James 89
Henry
  Dougald 156
Hobbs
  George 21
Hughenden
  Iris 189
  Robert 189
Huntley
  Henry 111
  Watson 110
  William 111
Hyndman
  A. W. 70
  Chas. A. 69
  James D. 69
  J. O. 70

Irving
    David P. 200

Jackson
    Catherine 77
    V. C. 77
Jenkins
    Albert N. 78
    Aubrey 78
    Ernest 78
    Nics. 157
Jetson. *See also* Judson
    Jacob 163
    John 163
    William 157, 163
Johnston
    William 96
Jones
    James Benjamin 154
    J. Walter 154
    Locke 96
    Maude 96
    Robert 83, 96, 152
    Sarah 96
    Willlam 152
Judson. *See also* Jetson
    Jacob 163
    John 163

Kelley
    Catherine 167
    Donald 167
Kempster
    F. 154
Kennedy
    George Rainy 187
Klein
    David 178
    John 178
    Karen 179

Laird
    James 18, 147, 165
    J. 19
    Margaret 165
    Polly 165
Lamond
    Alexander 144
Lane
    Franklin K. 76
Lard
    James 158
Laws
    William 158
Le Lacheur 164
Lindsay
    Lionel 77
Locke
    Margaret 152
Lockman
    Malcolm 117
    Peter 117
Lodge
    Frederick Dalgleish 190
Longworth
    F. 154
    J. 154

Macaulay. *See also* McAulay
    Aeneas (Æneas) 79, 124, 126.
        See also Angus Macaulay
    Alex. 117
    Alice 142, 171, 183
    Allen 117
    A. 128. *See also* Aeneas, Angus Macaulay
    Angus 14, 22, 48, 123, 124,
        125, 126, 129, 130, 133,
        134, 137, 138, 142
    Aulay 124, 126, 183
    Charlotte 16, 126, 141

Donald Cam (Blind Donald) 124
Donald 124, 171, 173, 183
Dugald 124
Ebenezer 142
Flora 141
John 141
Margaret 170
Mary 141
Zachary 126
MacCarthy
  Ella 75
MacCaskill
  Malcolm 126
Macdonald. *See also* MacDonald, McDonald
  Alexander Hector 69, 116
  Alexander 3, 70, 114, 174, 184, 185, 192
  Angus 114
  Annabella 174, 185
  Ann 68
  Archibald J. 73
  Catherine 69
  Daniel Alexander 70, 114
  Donald 57, 73, 114, 182
  Donald Gordon 72
  Don Hector 120
  Findlay 69, 70
  Flora 174, 185, 192, 193
  Florence 63
  Harold G. 73
  Hector 114
  Hugh 3, 174, 182, 185, 191
  Isabella 114
  James 3, 174, 182, 185
  James Mor 140
  Janet 185
  John D. 116
  John J. 63, 120
  Malcolm 119

Margaret 73, 182
Marion 174, 185
Mary Ann 114
Minnie 73
Murdoch R. 116
Neil 114
Norman 3, 58
Roderick 116, 191
Roderick E. 99
Rorie 192
Samuel 116
Soirle 141
Somerled 174, 185
MacDonald. *See also* Macdonald, McDonald
  Florence 182
  Hector 143
  James Jeremiah 73
  James 21, 73
  John 145
  Mary 140
  Samuel 117, 140
Macdonnell
  J. D. 154
MacDougall
  Angus 119
  Charles 119
  Duncan 119
  J. 120
MacEachern
  Archibald 119
  Charles 53
MacEachern (Bishop) 91

Machon 164
  Charles 200
Macinnis
  Daniel 120
Macintyre
  Hugh 187
  James 51, 184

Margaret 187
Peter 194
MacIver
  Donald 117
Mackay
  Alexander 87
Mackenzie. *See also* MacKenzie
  Alexander 182, 191, 192
  Ann 69
  David 69
  David Wallace 68
  Edith 68
  Eliza Margaret 63
  Findlay 68, 69
  Hector 108
  Isobell 182
  James W. 88
  Jane 191
  John 58
  Mary 63
  Roderick 119
MacKenzie. *See also* Mackenzie
  David 68
  Hector 83
  Kenneth 145
Mackinnon
  Archibald 53
  Artemas 73
  Charles 37
  Donald A. 73
  Donald 51, 93, 125, 143, 181, 190
  Jessie 69
  Mairi K. 93
  Margaret 73
  Sarah 171
  William 73
MacLaren
  Christene 169
  David Lawrence 170
  John 169, 170

Marjory 169
Maclean. *See also* MacLean
  Alexander 97, 99
  Angus 70
  Catherine 69
  Mary 70
  Murdoch 69, 143
  William 70
MacLean. *See also* Maclean
  Alexander 87, 187
  A. 70, 99, 154
  Angus A. 70, 99
  Angus 141
  Catherine Isabel 68, 70
  Flora 70, 99
  John 120
  Lachlan 120
  Lachlin 144
  Malcolm 120
  Samuel 116
  William 68, 99
MacLennan
  H. D. 163
  John 82, 84
Macleod. *See also* MacLeod, McLeod
  Alexander 49, 183, 184, 185
  Annabella 188
  Christine 172
  Donald 144
  Flora 191, 192
  Floretta 196
  John 191, 192
  Malcolm 30, 191, 192
  Margaret 185
  Marion 187
  Mary 124
  Murdo 185, 187
  Norman 196
  Roderick 126
  Sarah 30

MacLeod. *See also* Macleod,
    McLeod
  Adelaide 163
  Alex. 116
  Alexander 67, 82, 173
  Alexander R. 74
  Alexander William 178
  Alex. Jr. 118
  Alex 145
  Alex. Sr. 118
  Alex. Wm. 117
  Angus 69
  Annabella 173, 186
  Archibald 67
  Big Angus 30
  Christene 69
  Christiana 163
  Christina 177
  Christy 188
  Dame Flora 92
  Donald 117, 144, 145
  Donald A. 69
  Donald Ban 87
  Donald M. 116
  Duncan 72
  Floretta 67
  Helen 163
  James 69, 72
  John 118, 144, 191
  John F. 95
  John, Jr. 117
  John, Sr. 117
  Malcolm James 69
  Malcolm 72, 74, 116, 145
  Malcolm (Rory) 118
  Margaret 73, *married* Donald
      Gordon Macdonald
  Margaret 163
  Marion 171, 179
  Mary 163, 179
  Murdoch 67
  Murdo 173, 1858
  Neil 72, 73, 118
  Norman 67
  Roderick Charles 57
  Roderick (Ho ro) 117
  Roderick 73, 79, 118
  Ruth 178
  Samuel 53, 71, 72, 74
  Stella 163
  William 118, 163, 178
MacLeod of MacLeod (Mrs.,
      Chief of Clan MacLeod)
      92
Macmillan
  Malcolm 82
MacMillan
  Alexander 162
  Charles 159, 162
  Cyrus 71
  Frederick 162
  Hector Colonsay 71
  Henry Hyde 162
  Malcolm 71
  Maria 159, 162
  Melinda 162
MacMillan (U.E. Loyalist) 11
MacMorine
  Canon 77
  Morage 77
MacNeil
  John MacNeil 53
MacNeill
  John 54
Macneill (Doctor) 48

Macphail
  Andrew 77
  Catherine 77, 78
  Dorothy 77, *married* Lionel
      Lindsay
  Isabell 77

James Alexander 77
Janetta Clark 77
Jeffrey 77
John 77
John Andrew 76
John Goodwill 77
Margaret 78
Marion 77
Morage 77
William 76, 78, 95
William Matheson 77
Macphee. *See also* McFee, McPhee
  Samuel D. 87
Macpherson. *See also* MacPherson
  Daniel 99
  John 119, 144
  John James 74
  Kenneth 74
  Malcolm 119
  Martin 126
  Mary 76
  Neil 74
  Patton 98
MacPherson. *See also* Macpherson
  John 144
Macqueen
  Adelaide 190
  Alexander 58
  Alex. 3
  Alice 183, 187
  Angus 63, 172, 173, 177, 181, 183, 191, 192
  Angus Mor 181, 190
  Archibald 181, 182, 183, 191, 192
  Belle Irene 178
  Catherine 124, 183, 191
  Cedric Norman 188
  Christy 146
  Donald 69, 78, 126, 144, 172, 177, 182, 188, 192
  Dulcie 189
  Edmund 3
  Elizabeth 188
  Enid 189
  Ethlyn 189
  Ewen 171, 181, 190
  Flora Georgina 195
  Gertrude Georgina 77
  Henry Archibald Potter 195
  Isabell Burt 189
  James 173, 187
  Jane 191, 192
  Janet 173, 174, 186, 191
  Jessie Marshall 189
  John 144, 172, 183, 191, 194
  John Angus 63, 172, 177
  Kenneth 187, 188, 190
  Kenneth Og 191
  Lauchlan 191
  Leila 190
  Leslie Angus 188
  Malcolm A. 178
  Malcolm Frederick 188
  Malcolm 39, 58, 63, 172, 177, 187, 188, 190, 192, 193
  Malcolm Towers 189
  Mary 191
  Matilda Brown 64
  Murdo 183
  Orwell 190
  Peter 50, 58, 172
  Peter Alexander 188
  Peter Angus 188
  Peter Isaac 178
  Potter 190, 193, 194, 195
  Thomas Potter 190, 193, 194
  William 3, 126, 171, 180, 183, 187

Macrae. *See also* MacRae
  Donald 144
  Roderick 144
MacRae. *See also* Macrae
  Alex. 116
  Anne Campbell 62
  Anne D. 62
  Daniel 119
  David 119
  Donald 54, 62, 63, 116, 120, 143
  Donald A. 116
  Donald D. 120
  Elizabeth 161
  Evender 143
  Finlay 144
  Florence 62
  John 116, 145
  Martin 116
  Murdoch 116
  Roderick 63, 65, 119
  Roderick C. 62
  Sarah 63
  Thomas 119
MacSwain
  Allan 175
  Angus 66, 197
  Mary Ann 67, 197
MacTavish
  Christene 71
MacWilliam
  Charles 24
  John Robert 30
  Marquand 164
Marshall
  Anne Burgess 195
  John Long 195
Martin
  Alexander 171
  Alex 144
  Angus 75, 170, 172
  Anne 74
  Donald 145, 171, 172
  Donald Charles 171
  Herbert H. 172
  Hugh 75
  James Campbell 75
  John 171, 173
  John Samuel 75
  Katherine 172
  Kenneth 172
  Kenneth John 171
  Kenneth Montgomery 172
  Malcolm Campbell 75
  Margaret 64, 171, 172, 177, 188
  Marion 172
  Martin 144, 171
  Mary 69
  Peter 170, 171, 172
  Samuel 75, 78, 144
  Samuel Angus 75
Matheson
  Christine 191
  Lou 200
  Murdoch 191
McAulay. *See also* Macaulay
  Angus 127, 139
McArthur
  Alexander 145
McAulay
  Angus McAulay. *See* Angus Macaulay
McCrossen
  Barney 157

McDonald. *See also* Macdonald, MacDonald
  Alex. 97
  Hector 28
  John 144, 145, 157
  Murdoch 145

McEachern (priest) 15
MacFee 23. *See also* MacPhee, McPhee
McGinnis
  John 157
McInnes
  Donald 143
McInnis
  Alex. 120
McKenzie. *See also* Mackenzie, McKinzie, McKinsie
  Alexd. 144
  J. 147
  Roderick 27
McKinley
  F. F. 163
McKinsie
  John 144
McKinzie
  Kennat 144
McLennan. *See also* Maclennan
  John 54, 56, 85
McLeod. *See also* Macleod, MacLeod.
  Alexn. 144
  Catherine 146
  Donald 145
  Harry 144
  John 143, 163
  Murdoch 184
  Murdo 144
McLeod (squatter, Lot 57) 13
McMillan. *See also* Macmillan.
  Allan 144
  Angus 144
  Charlotte 199
  Elizabeth 72
  Hector 144
  James 144
  Malcolm 144
McMillan (early settler) 15

McNabb
  Catherine 84
McNeill
  Malcom 144
McNill
  Donald 144
McPhee. *See also* MacPhee, MacFee
  Donald 144
  Don. 157
McPhee (early settler) 14, 15
McPherson. *See also* Macpherson.
  Donald 144
McQuarry
  Hector 144
McRae. *See also* Macrae, MacRae
  Donald 64, 82
  Finlay 145
  Mary 69
  Roderick Campbell 64
Mellish
  Thomas 162, 172
  Thomas W. 173
Milbourne
  Colonel 99
  Margaret 99
Miller
  Elizabeth (nee Hayden) 161
  Jean 196
  Lemuel 161
Millwood
  Kathleen 189

Monlin
  John 158
Montgomery
  D. 154
  Isabella Macphail 63
  James 81

Moore
  Alice 172
  James St. Clair 68
Morison. *See also* Morrison
  Hector 144
Morris
  Win. 158
Morrison. *See also* Morison
  Anne 64
  Hayden 98
  Hector 119
  Kenneth 176
  Margaret 176
  Neil 64
Morton
  Brian Christopher 197
  H. W. 197
Mun
  John 144
  Malcolm 144
Munn
  Angus 144
  Edgar 26
  James 25, 26, 144
  Malcolm 25
Munro
  Alexander 174, 175, 186
  Andrew 173, 175
  Ann 175
  Annabella 186, 187
  Donald 48, 49, 175
  Elizabeth 187
  George 173, 174, 186
  George A. 175
  Isabella 187
  James 49, 173, 175, 177, 186, 188
  John 173, 175
  John Ban Mac Uilleam 173
  Kenneth 175
  Marion 49, 63, 177, 186

  Mary 175
  Mary Jane 68
  Nellie 48
  Thomas 175
  Thomas Boston 174, 175
  William 173
Murchison
  Alexander 115
  Angus J. 115
  Ann 70
  Donald 54, 143, 144, 170
  Donald D. 115
  Donald Og 70
  Donaldina 170
  Don Neil 120
  Etta 170
  Euphemia 30
  Hector J. 115
  Hector M. 115
  James 115
  John 113, 114, 115, 144
  John J. 115
  John James 115
  Malcolm 115
  Mary 70
  Murdoch M. 115
  Neil D. 115
  Neil M. 115
  Peter 115, 144
  Peter D. 115
  Roderick 115
  Samuel 142
Musick
  Adelaide 167
  Donald 167
  Gordon 167
  Gordon Waynes 167
  Henry 167
  Howard 167
  John 167
  Peter 157, 166, 167

Sarah 166
Thankful 166
Trevor Waye 167
William Henry 167
Mutch
  Benjamin 179
  George 179
Myers
  Richard 157

Neilsen
  Elizabeth Marshall 188
  James 188
Ness
  Angus 144
Nicholson. *See also* Nicolson
  Alexander Beaumont 66
  Alice 48
  Angus 73
  Annabella 179
  Arthur Stirling 179
  Daniel 179, 180
  Donald 27, 52, 108, 144, 162, 177, 187
  Elizabeth 178
  Evelyn 68
  Flora 66
  Gordon Daniel 179
  Hannah 180
  Isabella 28, 63
  Isabel 177
  James 66, 67
  James Gordon 68
  Jessie 48
  John 28, 48, 97, 126
  John Alexander 67
  John A. 66, 70, 119
  John C. 119
  Katherine 73
  Malcolm 117, 121
  Margaret 48

Peter 28, 49, 63, 180, 186
Roderick 120
Ruth 180
Samuel 116, 121
Sarah Louise 179
William Cedric 68
Nicholson of Steinshole.
    See Donald Nicholson
Nicolle 164
Nicolson. *See also* Nicholson
  Alexander 176, 191
  Donald 80, 144, 176, 191
  Isabella 177
  John 144, 176
  Malcolm 176
  Margaret 176
  Patrick 176
  Peter 176, 177
  Soirle 144

O'Cathan
  Conn 181
Odochardy. *See also* O'Dockerty, Dockerty
  Angus 144, 145
  Donald 144, 145
  Findlay 145
  Finlay 145
O'Dockerty. *See also* Odochardy, Dockerty
  Angus 145
Oliver
  Craig Robertson 197
  John 197
  Peter Fergus 197

Pendergast
  Tho. 157
Penrose
  Ethel 77

Pethick
 T. 154
Pipon
 E. P. 63
Pitcairn
 Blair 88
Pope
 Joseph 154
Potter
 John 193, 195
 Maria 193
 Thomas 190, 193, 194
Praught
 Frederick 157
 John 157, 166
Price
 Harry 178
 Sheila Hope 178

Quigley
 R. S. 88

Richards
 Thomas 110
Richardson
 Flora 179
Riley
 Harriet Murgatroyd 178
 John 121
Roberts 164
Robertson
 Alexander 196, 198
 Barbara 197
 Charles 197
 Esther 74
 Flora Johanna 197
 James 196
 Jessie 48, 198
 Judith Alida 197
 Lemuel 67
 Lemuel Fergus 196
 Margaret 198
 Mary 197
 Norman 67, 197
 Senator 48
 Thomas 156
 William 197
Rodger
 Thomas Anderson 88
Rosendahl
 Rita 189
Ross
 Angus 165
 Barbara Jane 178
 Catherine 116
 Daphne Isobel 178
 David 74, 177
 David Douglas 178
 Donald 144, 162
 Donald Cliffe 74
 Flora 162
 Janetta 162, 163
 John 144
 Margaret 163
 Marion Isabel 178
 Pamela Muriel 178
 Ross, Minister of Pictou 16
 Walter David 177
 Walter D. 64
 William 165
Rymal
 Catherine Albert 88

Schultze
 Fred 158
Schurman
 Jacob Gould 73
 Minnie 73
Scott
 Elizabeth 198
Selkirk (Earl of) 5, 6, 7, 8, 10,
   12, 13, 14, 15, 17, 18, 21,

22, 23, 24, 25, 26, 27, 28,
29, 39, 49, 52, 70, 81, 96,
97, 101, 108, 123, 142, 146,
147, 148, 153, 155, 156,
158, 161, 165, 168, 177
Sengie. *See* William MacLeod
Shaw
  Alex 120
  Allan 37, 143
  John 22
  Sarah 175
Simpson
  Hannah 152
Sinclair
  Alex. MacLean 87
  Donald M. 87
Singer
  Myrtle 179
Smith
  Catherine Moore 76
  Donald 97
  Elizabeth 197
  Findlay 76
  Finlay 97
  Frances Maud 66
  Francis W. 66
  Henry 66
  Isaac 154
  James 149
  Jeremiah 197
  Joseph 157
  Samuel 149
Spence
  John David Macdonald 70
Spraggens 98
Steinshole 26, 27, 28, 49, 86, 95, 162, 176, 177. *See also* Donald Nicholson
  Patrick. *See* Peter Nicolson
Stewart
  Alex. Sinclair 87

  Alice 48
  Arthur Stewart 185
  Catherine 141
  Charles 143, 144
  Clarence 48
  Donald 144
  Maria Isabel 154
Stewart (sheriff) 16
Stoddart
  Marjorie 146

Taylor
  Alma 178
Throckmorton
  John 158
Throckmorton of Cherry Valley 20
Turner
  Leonard 179
Tweedy
  Anne 200
  Cephas Barker 199
  Elizabeth 200
  George 199, 200, 201
  George Joseph 199
  Harry 200
  John 166, 199, 200
  Joseph 166, 200
  Penelope 200
  Robert 200
  Thomas 199, 200
  Weldon 199

Van Niderstine
  John 158, 166
Vessey
  Edith 170
Vickerson
  Conrad 198
  Emma 196, 198

Wadland
  Wallace 88
Wagner
  Susannah 166
Welling
  H. J. 197
Welsh
  William 110
Whyt
  John 134
Whyte
  John (Major General) 129
Williams
  James 25
Wisener
  Ann (nee Hayden) 162
  Catherine 169

Wolrige-Gordon
  John 93
  Patrick 93
Wood
  William 157
Wright (son of Surveyor General) 16

Young
  Angus 119
  Ann 62
  Thomas 119
  William 158

OTHER WORKS OF GENEALOGY AVAILABLE FROM
SELKIRK STORIES

Skye Pioneers and "The Island" (1929) by Malcolm A. Macqueen.

The MacLeods of Prince Edward Island (1983, rev. 2017) by Harold S. MacLeod.

www.ingramcontent.com/pod-product-compliance
Lightning Source LLC
Chambersburg PA
CBHW052054110526
44591CB00013B/2210